THE WONDERS OF THE
AMALFI
and Capri Ischia Naples Pompeii Sorrento
COAST

WHITE STAR PUBLISHERS

THE WONDERS OF THE
AMALFI
and Capri Ischia Naples Pompeii Sorrento
COAST

Text
Paolo Rubino

Layout
Paola Piacco

Translation
Neil Frazer Davenport

CONTENTS

✳

1 The dome of the church of San Luca, from among the fishermen's houses of Praiano, looks out towards the enchanting bay of Positano.

2-3 The Ravello area, along the Amalfitana coast displays presents the typical landscape of the Amalfitana and Sorrentine coasts with towering ribs of rock topped with green that dive sheer into the deep blue of the sea.

4-5 So famous as to become "the Stacks" by antonomasia, the three enormous rocks of Capri are, from left to right, 341, 266, and 358 feet tall.

6-7 The imposing Vanvitellian palace at Caserta built at the behest of Charles III of Bourbon, stands out amid the vegetation of its vast park that grazes the new town and climbs towards the Great Cascade.

8-9 At Marina della Corricella, on the island of Procida, time seems to have stopped and crystallized the ancient fishing village with its characteristic wooden boats waiting to sail out in the evening by the light of their lampare or fishing lanterns.

10 This delicate portrait of a young girl named Saffo was discovered at Pompeii. It is now conserved in the National Archaeological Museum of Naples, together with collections of other relics found in the Roman cities buried by the eruption of Vesuvius.

11 Campania is a region of strong contrasts not only in everyday life and history, but also in the colors of the rugged rocks of the Amalfitana coast that, baked by the sun, plunge into clear waters.

ISBN 88-544-0086-6
Reprints:
1 2 3 4 5 6   09 08 07 06 05

Printed in Korea

12 top *The historic center of Naples preserves centuries-old traditions concealed amid the multicolored lanes where, in the ancient craft workshops of Via San Gregorio Armeno, the art of making terracotta nativity scenes and shepherds has been handed down through the generations.*

12 bottom *The majestic dome in cast iron and glass of the Galleria Umberto I, the city-center salon of late nineteenth century Naples, was inspired by the masterpieces of Parisian architecture.*

INTRODUCTION

N aples and its surrounding region, a province called Campania, is a land in which the beauty of landscapes forged by volcanic might is married to the richness of a lengthy history. Closely bound to the sea, to the blue of the Tyrrhenian, its coast a jumbled patchwork of rocks and greenery, Campania proudly defends the traditions and flavors of the small inland agricultural communities, set amidst vineyards and chestnut trees. It is a land to be experienced, to be savored slowly, with its myriad atmospheres waiting to be discovered one by one.

Campania is a land of strong contrasts. The concrete expanses of an immense metropolitan area have failed to overwhelm the timeless hamlets, towns, and cities. Although the towns have kept abreast of the latest developments and are casting an eye towards the future, they have not obscured the most precious and simplest treasures of an ancient heritage, the flavors of a traditional cuisine, the appeal of magical stories handed down over the centuries, religious sentiment entwined with the color of strong popular beliefs, the secrets of craftsmen, and a world enclosed within numerous corners of city lanes, of fishing villages, and of country villages. The pearls of international tourism shine brightly – Capri, Sorrento, Positano – but a thousand other surprises wait to delight the senses. Going back in time, following the traces of thousands of years of history, one plunges into the infinite itineraries of an immense monumental heritage. The cities of the Greeks or the traces of even older civilizations, the villas of the Roman emperors, the Naples of the kings, and the unique marvel of the Roman cities petrified by the eruption of Vesuvius are all captivating. It is a difficult region to decribe: a multicolored mosaic of countless tiny pieces, each one inspiring a different reaction that is difficult to describe and that will never be the same for everyone. This is Campania, with its crucible of sensations waiting to be gathered.

This book follows two paths. It brings together two different feelings, two ways of seeing, and two ways of describing the same land. The images are those which have captured the imagination of a photographer who discovers views, panoramas, cities, atmospheres, glimpses of everyday life, monuments, curiosities, well-known scenes of beauty and treasures awaiting discovery. She looks at everything for the first time, arriving from afar, taking photographs at the very moment in which she

12-13 *Naples seen from Posillipo unfolds in all its glory. Castel Sant'Elmo dominates the city that descends gently towards the bay, from the waters of which rise the tuff walls of Castel dell'Ovo.*

13 bottom *Naples lives in the myriad faces of its people, such as this ageing greengrocer weighing goods for a client on an antique brass scale.*

experiences sensations that for her are new, capturing the colors and plays of light and shadow, and freezing images filtered by the highly individual sensibility of an artist. The story is that of a journalist, a Neapolitan whose eyes roam over this land each and every day, which is not to say that she presumes to know and understand it in all its complexity and its many varied aspects. Instead she tries to discover something more, with the curiosity of a reporter, yet without the presumption of intending to describe everything, but simply trying to advance a short way beyond the curtain of an everyday life that dazzles and

14 top The remains of Cuma, the first Greek colony on the Italian mainland, founded eight centuries before Christ, testify to a past rich in stories and characters.

14 bottom A view of the Roman city of Pompeii brings to mind the tragedy that came about on August 24, 79 A.D., when the eruption of Vesuvius buried the city beneath a mantle of ashes and debris.

distracts, and to search out moments of real life, freeze the ferment and the simplicity of popular tradition, review and reinterpret daily life in the light of episodes of a significant history that has left indelible signs.

Four chapters. Four itineraries. Just four ideas like those anyone may come up with as they set out to explore this region, following imaginative whims or plotting the routes that appeal to them the most.

In this land of fire: volcanoes have imposed colors, shapes, and history. Campania Felix, fertile and luxuriant thanks to the ashes of a thousand eruptions, is still dominated by the dozing volcano Vesuvius, fumaroles, incandescent craters, bubbling hot spring waters, and coasts of tuff and rocky islands produced by ancient eruptions.

Naples has a thousand stories to tell, with stories of kings and queens, and the stories of a gregarious people. It offers churches, palaces, piazzas, alleys, imagination, colors, and flavors, culture and popular tradition. It boasts a rich and complex history, which is not simply the history of books, of the ancient civilizations, of the different influences of numerous outside powers, but also that of everyday life. There is a whole world to be discovered here, with unique and unmistakable characters.

The sea has always been a priceless resource, and it represents another important chapter in the history of this region. Two coasts famous throughout the world, that of Sorrento and that of Amalfi, enchant with their tiny villages set amidst greenery and sheer cliffs. The islands are the pearls of the Bay of Naples. And further south, natural atmospheres xan be discovered, on an itinerary far from the well-beaten tourist track, among the authentic beauties of the Cilento national park.

Naples, beautiful, steeped in history, unjustly overshadows other cities with all their treasures and their own important past to recount. Between Salerno on the coast to the south and Caserta to the north, one can explore the spirit of this region of southern Italy, getting to know something about the provincial capitals, entering into the authentic life of small towns, less well known and not so much as touched by tourism, passing through hills and green mountain woods, while glimpsing jealously guarded traditions and a simple lifestyle.

Images embellish the text as well as the photographs. Simple snapshots of a rich, broad, multifaceted reality. The two authors have absorbed and attempt to relate the emotions generated by this land. But Campania is out there, waiting to be discovered.

14-15 The last rays of sunset lend warmth to the colors of the Temple of Ceres, one of the three Doric temples at Paestum on the Bay of Salerno where, in the seventh century BC, the Greeks founded Poseidonia, a colony dedicated to Neptune.

15 bottom The Campano amphitheater at Santa Maria Capua Vetere challenged the Coliseum of Rome for its size and elegance. It was subsequently destroyed by the Saracens.

16-17 The theater scene of the mosaic in the House of the Tragic Poet is one of the most fascinating relics from Pompeii now conserved in the National Archaeological Museum of Naples.

18-19 The Temple of Neptune is dedicated to the Greek god, as was the whole of the colony of Poseidonia that housed it. The building, the largest of Paestum's three Doric temples, is built of local travertine stone that in the sunlight reveals characteristic golden tones.

14

20-21 Sunny Positano, stands on the southern slopes of the Lattari Mountains.

22-23 The Amalfi Coast, sheltered from the northern winds, enjoys a rather fortunate location.

LAND OF FIRE
TUFA, LAVA AND CRATERS

24 top The Sacellum of the Augustalis, on the coast at Miseno, has in part been dragged below sea level by the slow bradyseismic movement of the earth.

24 center top Lake Lucrino occupies the bottom of a crater.

24 center bottom The Solfatara of Pozzuoli is the base of a dormant volcano.

Campania is a land born out of fire. Fire is an integral part of its image and history. A land of volcanoes, the gentle hills are lapped by the sea while a breeze mitigate the scorching midday sun. Ashes and lapilli have contributed to the precious gift of a rare fertility that, already noted two thousand years ago, led to the area being known as Campania Felix, or "happy, fortunate, and generous country." Eruptions, long ago, created the towering coastline that falls sheer to the deep blue sea and painted the landscape with the dark black of hard volcanic rock and the pale yellow of friable tuff.

In this land of sailors and fishermen, the people still set their nets at sunset and pull them in at dawn, laboring in their traditional rowing boats cradled by the waves of the Gulf of Naples. A land of farmers, and ancestral and immortal traditions. In the interlocking streets of the popular quarters of the towns and villages as well as the great city of Naples, the atmosphere is charged with solid human relationships in a climate of intimacy and solidarity that elsewhere survives only the smallest of villages.

The Neopolitans are simple people but their home is also a land of kings and queens. Today, it proudly recalls a leading role in history and claims its rightful place among the prominent tourist and cultural attractions. Noble, it is ready to share its inherited masterpieces from bygone eras of glory, the appeal of its strong popular traditions, and the wonders of a vigorous, unique landscape. Over the centuries the capital has developed a culture that in a web of distant influences carries the indelible marks of a hundred civilizations and a hundred dominations. Here, landed the ancient Greeks who found not a desert but the lively intelligence of the people of Italica. Here, the Romans founded great cities. Seafarers and merchants encountered the civilizations of the Far East. Here, powerful lords ruled and here they handed over the sceptre to kings and emperors arriving from distant lands.

The hills are ancient volcanoes. Crowned by towering, sheer crags, those lakes, those bays, those quiet valleys are a myriad of extinct craters. The islands rose from the sea bed, lifted by the fury of eruptions before breaking up and plunging back into the abysses to create spectacular rock walls. On the other hand the volcano Vesuvius doze, powerful, and threatening at the shoulder of towns that recount histories of destruction and proud revival. Rivers of incandescent lava and slicks of mud and ashes have frozen time, buried life, and erased entire cities. In a treasure chest of earth and stone, they have enwrapped and conserved the houses, theaters, and temples that, today restored at Herculaneum and Pompeii after

24 bottom and 24-25 Vesuvius is a constant threat for the coast of the Bay of Naples. The scars of black rock on its slopes testify to the violence of the lava flows.

26-27 Hundreds of buildings are spread across the Sarno plain, north of the Lattari Mountains. On the right in the photo, moving inland, Pompeii can be discerned.

centuries of obscurity, are the most dramatic, mysterious, and fascinating testimony to life two thousand years ago.

Puffs of steam rank with the unmistakable odor of sulfur heat the stones and impregnate the air of the Campi Flegrei (Phlegraean Fields). "Flegrei," or burning, as the Greeks called it, refers to strip of land that, follows the coast of the Tyrrhenian Sea northwards as far as the Cape Miseno lighthouse, high on a spur of rock jutting into the sea off the island of Procida and, ancient Cuma perched on a green hill a little higher up the coast which gaze out towards the horizon beyond the island of Ischia. The earliest colonists had no doubts about those contorted and imposing rocks, and those vapors cracking the land and embracing ancient craters in a sinister fog. This corner of Campania with its lunar landscape, could hardly be other than the site of the mythical battle between the gods and the titans who had dared to climb Olympus as mentioned by Homer and Virgil. They called this the "Land of Myth" in which every stone recounts fantastic adventures and suggestive stories, and where the Roman patricarchs, enchanted by the rebellious nature, built their most luxurious villas.

28-29 Each year Ischia welcomes thousands of visitors. This "pearl of the Mediterranean," also known as the "Green Island," was destroyed by the volcano Arso in 1301. However, the fertility of its land and the properties of its mineral waters and thermal springs renowned throughout the world exist thanks to the eruptions and the volcanic rock.

28 bottom The port of Ischia, a small volcanic crater, was transformed into a safe natural harbor at the behest of Ferdinand II who in 1854 ordered the demolition of the rock wall that obstructed movements to and from the sea.

The first colonists landed on the coast of Ischia, which they baptised Pithecusa. The etymology is debatable. It may mean The Island of Vases because colorful clay was worked there, in ancient times just as it is today. Or, it may refer to the Island of Monkeys, the island of the mythical Cercopi who, inhabitants of the fiery inferno of volcanic lands, found their ideal home here. Ischia is the largest of the pearls of the Bay of Naples and is known as the "green island" thanks to luxuriant vegetation challenging the rock-scorching heat of the southern sun. Fire has blessed the island with thermal waters that flow from over a hundred springs. They can be found on the seashore, among the fumaroles of the Maronti beach and the pebbles of Soceto, and at Cava Scura, in the ancient pools the Romans carved into the tuff to create improvised baths. Today, in the innumerable thermal spas and captivating gardens that

29 top The Maronti beach is one of Ischia's most characteristic features. Fumaroles rise constantly from the sand and the water, and in the background are the white houses of Sant'Angelo, an old and evocative fishing village.

29 bottom The village of Forio on Ischia faces onto the blue waters of the Mediterranean. The

vegetation surrounding it includes grape vines on the slopes of the hills where the island's most highly prized wine is produced.

30-31 Within a perimeter of about 22 miles and contained within 18 square miles of surface area, Ischia's terrain is more rolling and welcoming to the north than on its wild southern part.

climb from the sea amid the greenery of steep hillsides, exotic plants and flowers a step away from the cliffs grow together with olive and lemon trees, and large basins collect the water as it gushes from the springs with varying temperatures and mineral contents. There are also the beaches and solariums. These self-contained corners of paradise with their exotic feel sit happily among the colors of the Mediterranean. The springs are today the most valuable resource of an island loved by Germans and North Europeans, an island that can count on an uninterrupted flow of tourists to fill its many hotels overlooking the sea or nestling in the cooler hills.

Tourism, however, has not taken away any of the appeal of fishing villages such as Sant'Angelo, with its cobbled lanes climbing away from the sea and small houses clustered behind a minuscule port. High on Monte Epomeo, the traditional farming way of life is barely touched by the invasion of vacationers. Specialities of the region, such as bucatini with a rabbit sauce, can be eaten up in the hills but also on the cliffs overlooking the sea, in any of the small restaurants that can only be reached by water. Seen from the sea, the bold and mysterious forms molded by the lava present a magnificent spectacle. Those steps carved into the tuff are impossibly narrow strips of land torn from the tumbling hillsides, each terrace boasting a row of ancient vines. This is heroic agriculture, a combination of back-breaking labor and passion that with the felicitous marriage of volcanic earth and the hot sun of Ischia, gives rise to fine wine. Hospitable cellars, a sample of local flavors, and a glass of the island's typical white wine are to be found in the Forio area below the great rock, "the home of the great serpent, custodian of the island" according to ancient folklore. This is located in the hills behind the village where for centuries, in a little white church perched on the rocks, the womenfolk of fishermen and sailors, both mothers and wives, have prayed to the Madonna of the Shrine of Deliverance so that their loved ones may return home safely. The Aragonese castle a fortified village on a small island linked to Ischia by a long bridge built at the behest of Alfonso of Aragon extends a symbolic hand in the direction of the neighboring islands of Vivara and Procida, one beside the other, separated only by an old, broken-rimmed crater invaded by the sea.

32 top Crafts on Ischia have a long tradition, a perpetuation of ancient gestures, as in the case of the manufacture of cane baskets.

32 bottom The small fishing boats in Forio's minuscule harbor are waiting for evening before sailing out to set their nets.

32-33 The Aragonese Bridge links the village of Ischia Ponte to the island on which Ischia Castle is sited. A fortified wall encloses a maze of buildings from various ages around the ruins of the fourteenth century Cathedral of Our Lady of the Assumption.

33 bottom left The waves break close to the houses of Ischia Ponte, the oldest part of the commune of Ischia. It is one of the island's six administrative districts, the others being, Barano, Casamicciola Terme, Forio, Lacco Armeno, and Serrara Fontana.

33 bottom right The white shrine of Santa Maria del Soccorso stands on the rocks at Forio, protecting the Ischians far from home. The Madonna watches over the emigrants and leads the fishermen home, defending them from the sea's fury.

Green, with not a brick in sight, the small island of Vivara defends its patrimony of rare vegetation reflected in a crystalline sea. It was here that struck by the color of its shrubs the ancient Greeks elected the myrtle as a plant sacred to Apollo. Procida timidly shuns the chaos and notoriety of international tourism. There are only a few hotels and shops. It is little more than a stone's throw away, but so different from crowded Ischia and ultra-chic Capri. It is an island of fishermen with clusters of pastel-colored houses, no two alike, that overlook small bays with imposing walls of tuff while dark lava flows at their backs. The volcanic craters, over the centuries a natural shelter for fishing boats, are today amphitheaters of stone embracing small seaside villages. There is Marina di Chiaiolella, below the peak of Punta della Palombara, and Corricella, the most attractive of these villages with its patchwork of cottages that climb steeply from the dockside in a labyrinth of arches, doorways, steps, and lanes. With no cars and no roads, what little space is available on the shore is devoted to the wooden boats drawn up almost to the doors of the houses and to the drying of fishing nets which the expert hands of the villages' elder citizens spend hours repairing with needle, thread, and infinite patience. In this tiny, isolated corner, cut off from the rest of the world and, untouched by modern-day rhythms, the French writer Alfonse De Lamartine encountered the beautiful Graziella, a young girl dressed in red, her head covered with a scarf of silk and gold sequins, the typical islanders' costume. Enchanted, he took her with him into the imaginary world of his novels, dedicating the pages of a heart-rending love story to her. Each evening the lamps of the large wooden fishing boats are lit, a constellation of white lights sailing out to sea to fish until dawn. As the deep red sun sets behind the fortress of yellow stone, the fishermen turn for one last glance at the houses and, higher up, the church clinging to the edge of a sheer drop to which they direct a last prayer, the sea caves, and higher still, the abbey of San Michele, patron saint of the island. This is the village of Terra Murata, the oldest of the coastal hamlets, set on the highest point possible. It offered an inaccessible natural fortress where the Procidians sought refuge from the Saracen invasions.

Today the scene is dominated by the skeleton of the old, abandoned jail. The oldest of traditions are still repeated. On the evening of Maundy Thursday, the hooded monks descend from the rock carrying the Cross on their shoulders and slowly march from one church to the next. The following day the whole village accompanies Our Lady of Sorrows in the procession behind the figure of the dead Christ. Hour upon hour, with immense fatigue, these members of an ancient congregation dressed in white and turquoise tunics, carry allegorical floats secretly constructed in the entrances of the old houses. Large and extremely heavy wood and paper-mache representations of sacred scenes, and the riches of the island such as fresh fish, bread, huge lemons, and rabbits of the countryside are offered in thanks.

34-35 The maze of houses and steps in the port of Corricella enlivens the most suggestive corner of the island of Procida. From the top of the hill, the old prison hides the village of Terra Murata.

34 bottom left Seen from above, the irregular and sinuous shapes of the bay of Procida betray its origin as four large volcanic craters.

34 bottom right An elderly fisherman patiently repairs his nets on the pier at Corricella on the island of Procida.

35 top right The houses of the fishing village of Corricella on Procida compose a picturesque and colorful mosaic overlooking the sea.

35 bottom right The luminous dome of the church of Santa Maria delle Grazie, high above the port of Corricella, towers over the houses of Procida.

On the other side of a narrow stretch of sea, the coastline features the surreal traces of ancient eruptions. History, legend, and nature are entwined in a landscape of fantastic imagery. Cuma is the oldest ancient Greek colony on the Italian mainland. There is soft tuff rock below the trees growing a stone's throw from the sea and six centuries before Christ a long tunnel was dug there. It was supposedly the cavern of the immortal Sybilla who, when interrogated over the years by those about to embark on perilous enterprises, consulted the gods and made prophecies never disproved by the facts. The secret was enclosed in the few words of skilfully constructed phrases,

the kinds of ambiguities that still today, in reference to this ancient legend, we call "sybilline." Hard volcanic rock a little higher up supports the Acropolis, the Temple of Apollo, the Temple of Jupiter, statues, colonnades, and terraces overlooking the sea.

Cape Miseno is an imposing spur where, according to Virgil, Miseneum, the herald of Aeneas, was buried. And here, according to Strabo, there was the land of the Lestrigone giants who by launching huge rocks drove off Ulysses and his companions, all of whom escaped except for Miseneum who was attacked by Antiphas.

Those rocks were, so large that they fell with sufficient force to carve this labyrinth of bays out of the sea-polished tuff. The series of small and large craters compose a backdrop of peaks and caves. Here in the Waters of Death, so-called because they are as still as a lake and sheltered from the open sea, the Greek vessels and then the ancient Romans' fleet of triremes enjoyed the benefits of a secure harbor. The fleet was provided with water by the enormous Piscina Mirabilis, a cistern carved into the tuff of Punta del Poggio during the Augustan period and linked to the distant hills by the Serino aqueduct. The cavea of the Roman theater overlooks the sea from Punta Scarparella and, the walls of the now extinct sumptuous Roman villas still stand. Never wholly extinguished volcanoes still cause carbon dioxide and hydrogen sulphide to rise from the water and emanate from the walls of the "Grotta dello Zolfo" (Sulfur Cavern). Nearby Baia (named after Baios, a companion of Ulysses who was buried and is honored here), is dominated by the castle, another fortress overlooking the sea, that in the sixteenth century the viceroy Don Pedro of Toledo had constructed over the ruins of the Roman palace of the Caesars in order to defend the coast from the attacks of the corsairs. Also at Baia, the water bubbled and gushed from a hundred springs. Behind the little port the fact was confirmed by the excavation of the most luxurious thermal baths of ancient Rome, three large halls that were so beautiful the first archaeologists to examine them thought they were temples. The consul Gnaeus Cornelius Scipione treated his debilitating arthritis here, according to Livius. For the great Horace, this was the most enchanting bay in the world. Perhaps this was why Licinius Crassus, Caius, Caesar, Pompey, Varro, Cicero, and Hortensius all built great villas here for their seaside vacations. Caligula even had a floating bridge constructed in order to facilitate crossing the two-mile stretch of sea separating Baia from Pozzuoli.

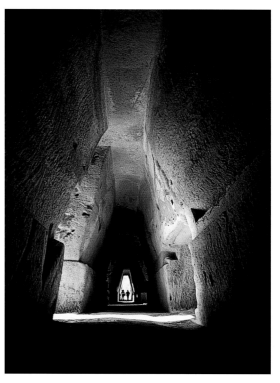

36-37 The white lighthouse of Cape Miseno stands out on the impressive walls of tuff falling sheer to the sea. These cliffs are the remains of a volcanic cone destroyed by the sea over the course of the centuries.

36 bottom The Campi Flegrei to the south of Cuma included Lake Lucrino, separated from the coast by a thin strip of land. The volcano Mount Nuovo rises on the horizon.

37 top right The coastline of the Campi Flegrei winds towards Cuma, to the north, and separates Lake Fusaro, a coastal lagoon seen on the right in this photo, from the sea.

37 center right The Sybil of Cuma made her predications in a room at the end of a long gallery. The Hall of the Sybil was begun in the sixth century B.C. at the foot of the acropolis of one of the oldest Greek colonies.

37 bottom right The Romans carved out the Piscina Mirabile, a great cistern linked to the Serino aqueduct, out of the tuff of Punta del Poggio. It supplied water to the fleet in the port of Miseno.

38 top Lake Aveno, a safe haven for the ships of the Roman fleet which entered by way of a tunnel and a canal, was in the past considered to be the gateway to hell and an appropriate place for sacrifices to the gods.

38 bottom To the south of the Campi Flegrei, the coast of Naples is also characterized by evidence of the ancient volcanoes. The islet of Nisdia, in fact, located in front of the abandoned industrial area of Bagnoli, is the wall of a crater open towards the city.

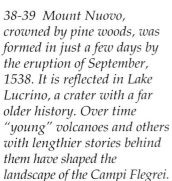

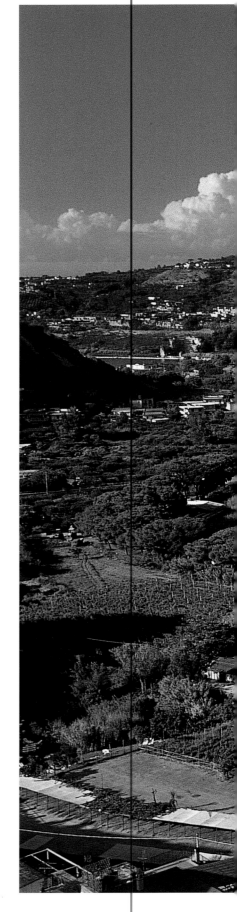

Two thousand years ago, bradyseism, the slow seismic movement that pushes land up or down, dragged Roman villas and towns below sea level. Just a few years ago, the earth stirred once again, rising slowly and causing grave damage to the houses of Pozzuoli, with thousands of families forced to leave the evocative lanes of the historic town center and move to new, anonymous, modern-day accomodations.

The suggestive Rione Terra, an ancient fortress overlooking the sea, is now nothing but a ghost town. Thus have fire and volcanoes shaped the life of the distant past and conditioned that of today.

Kept away by the acidic exhalations, birds steer clear of the crater lake of Averno, described in the Aeneid as the gateway to hell. This is the land of the Cimmerians where the sun never shines, as described in the Odyssey. For the ancients it was hell itself, a propitious site for rituals and sacrifices. The Romans dug canals to link it to the sea and made it a port. It lies close to Lake Lucrino in the hills that witnessed the slaying of Agrippa and where the "Stufe di Nerone," or Nero's Ovens, can be found. Here, the water runs at 189°F, with vapor at 140°F, just as when the Romans dug these caves to form sudatoria with beneficial therapeutic properties.

Only a slim strip of land and sand divides Lake Lucrino from the sea. The remains of Roman walls are still visible on the coast, while on an island linked to the mainland by a narrow bridge stands the Casino Reale, built during the eighteenth century when the lake became a hunting reserve of King Ferdinand IV of Bourbon.

Not far away is Solfatara, the crater that among many others in the Campi Flegrei, has never ceased to rumble and appears to be unwilling to allow itself to fall deeper into sleep. The crater is entered via a gap open towards the sea, first through greenery and then along a suggestive path across the belly of the volcano, a lunar landscape with spurting vapor, bubbling mud, rocks painted yellow by sulfur and ground that is hot to the touch.

38-39 Mount Nuovo, crowned by pine woods, was formed in just a few days by the eruption of September, 1538. It is reflected in Lake Lucrino, a crater with a far older history. Over time "young" volcanoes and others with lengthier stories behind them have shaped the landscape of the Campi Flegrei.

39 bottom left The Aragonese castle of Baia, built on the remains of a Roman villa that tradition has it belonged to Julius Caesar and that was probably part of the villa of Nero, overlooks the sea to the south. The building now houses the Archaeological Museum of the Campi Flegrei.

39 bottom right The statues of Vespasian and Titus have been placed within a reconstruction of the facade of the sacellum at Miseno in the Archaeological Museum of the Campi Flegrei.

History and the sea are the twin spirits of the town of Pozzuoli, entwined amid glimpses of the remote past and everyday life. The great Flavian amphitheater, and the columns of the Temple of Serapis can be seen against the background of the port crowded with wooden fishing boats while the deafening cries of the fishmongers rise each morning from the huge fish market. Naples is not far away, beyond another small crater with its flank sinking into the waves to form the suggestive bay of Porto Paone on the island of Nisida. Between the island and the great city rises the high tuff cliff of Cape Posillipo with its caves and spurs

of rock polished by the waves. The Romans dug long tunnels here to reach villas and theaters built overlooking the sea, such an isolated and inaccessible area having been chosen because of its immense beauty. Vesuvius dominates the bay with its threatening mouth of fire. The great volcano sleeps but is not extinct. Today, it looms over a sea of houses, uncontrolled development that shows neither respect for nor fear of the mountain's destructive potential.

Here and there, at the foot of the giant, traces of a relatively recent noble past still survive. The elegant eighteenth century villas stretch one after the other along the ancient and prestigious Via Regia whose splendors led to it being rebaptised as the Miglia d'Oro, or Golden Mile. Nearby, at Portici, Charles III of Bourbon challenged the flaming mountain when he built a palace at its foot. "God, the Virgin Mary, and San Gennaro will protect it," he said to prophets of impending destruction. The noble families followed his lead and built splendid homes. The gateway, the porticoes, the loggia, and the belvedere, repeat the design in a suggestive composition that from the summit of Vesuvius descends to the sea. Villa Signorini, Villa Campolieto, and higher up, on the slopes of Vesuvius itself, Villa delle Ginestre, home of Giacomo Leopardi, are all splendid examples.

The eruption of 1794 spared the Via Regia but destroyed Torre del Greco. Here, sixty-seven years later, on December 8, 1861, the day dedicated to the Virgin Mary, when everything was ready for the procession that had been held for three centuries, Vesuvius' sinister rumbling was heard once again.

The earth shook to such a degree that buildings collapsed while the people prayed for the intercession of the Virgin Mary. Miraculously, the river of fire stopped at the town gates. Torre del Greco has never forgotten that day nor the debt it owes. Ever since then, on the 8th of December each year, the statue of the Virgin is carried through the petal-strewn streets of the town by hundreds of the faithful on an imposing platform of wood and paper-mache that is destroyed and remade annually. The lava flow of 1906 stopped just a short distance from the town at Bosco Trecase and at Torre Annunziata where, every 22nd of October, prayers are offered to the Madonna of the Snows in thanks and in the hope of avoiding further eruptions.

Torre del Greco is famous throughout the world for its working of coral and its cameos. This is the traditional craft heritage of artists skilled in the sculpting of exquisite bas-reliefs from branches of red coral and the fine engraving of fragments of large shells. There are dozens of workshops and ninety percent of the coral worked throughout the world passes through them. Higher up the slopes, only the yellow flowers of the broom alleviate the black of Vesuvius' cones. Today, the area has been declared a Natural Park climb across, lava and threading your way along deep volcanic scars up to the rim of the great crater, it is possible to see a breathtaking panorama.

40-41 The statue of the Blessed Mary carried on the shoulders of the faithful of Torre del Greco through the town under a rain of petals celebrates the intervention that on June 8, 1861, saved the community from the erupting Vesuvius.

40 bottom The old port of Pozzuoli and the ancient parish of Rione Terra still show the signs of the bradyseism that raised the level of the pier in 1970.

41 top right The ruins of the Temple of Serapis, so named because a statue of the Greco-Egyptian god was found there, was the macellum of ancient Puteoli, the present-day Pozzuoli.

41 center right This aerial view shows the size of the great Flavian Amphitheater encircled by the houses of Pozzuoli. Tradition has it that it was built during the era of Vespasian.

41 bottom right Vesuvius, a fearful source of fire that for years has stood dormant overlooking the Bay of Naples, still assumes a threatening air when the sky is obscured by clouds.

42 left The volcano's cone looms over Via Stabiana, the old road that crosses the heart of Pompeii, cutting the city in two from Porta del Vesuvio to Porta di Stabia, heading towards the towns of the Sorrentine peninsula.

42 top right The crowds filled the terraces to watch the ludi gladiatori in the great amphitheater at Pompeii. The stadium was built on the edge of the city to prevent the tide of spectators from disrupting daily life.

42 bottom right In this aerial view of Pompeii, the Gladiator's Barracks, in the foreground, the big amphitheater, and the odeion, used for musical performances and political reunions, stand out.

Vesuvio also recalls some of the most tragic pages of Roman history when whole cities were smothered and buried by the volcano's fury, then petrified over time and rediscovered centuries later. The ruins of Pompeii, submerged by raining ashes, and those of Herculaneum, swamped by a flood of mud and lava, together with the villas of Oplonti and Stabiae, present dramatic and evocative scenes.

Lava and raining ash brought death. It did not take long, just a few hours, for an eruption to cast its spell and freeze history and everyday life at dawn on the twenty-fourth of August in the year 79 A.D.. A sinister grumbling echoed in the belly of the volcano.

Then the rumble of a thousand thunderbolts shook the earth as the mountain exploded. Over the sea, from Cape Miseno where he was in command of the Roman fleet, Pliny the Elder could see the houses of Herculaneum, Oplonti, and further to the south, Pompeii. He felt the earth shake and saw the sun disappear behind the cloud of smoke rising from

43 The ashes produced by the eruption of Vesuvius buried the Temple of Apollo while restoration work made necessary by the violent earthquake of the year 62 A.D. was still underway. The bronze statue of Apollo with his bow is a copy of the original, today conserved in the National Archaeological Museum of Naples.

44-45 Via di Stabia, or Stabia Street, cuts this magnificent view of Pompeii taken from the southeast diagonally, almost vertically with respect to the theater and the odeion. Via dell'Abbondanza (Abundance Street) is visible in the middle of the photo.

Vesuvius. Spurred by his curiosity as an enthusiastic naturalist, he headed in that direction. When he heard that people were in danger, he did not hesitate and died a hero's death. The account of those hours is contained in two letters that his seventeen-year-old grandson , Pliny the Younger, wrote to the historian Tacitus...

The closer to the coast they traveled, the hotter and denser the ashes that fell on them, and pumice and black stones burnt and shattered by the fire fell... [There was] a black and frightening cloud torn by snaking, dazzling tongues of flame... There were those who for fear of death invoked death itself. Many raised

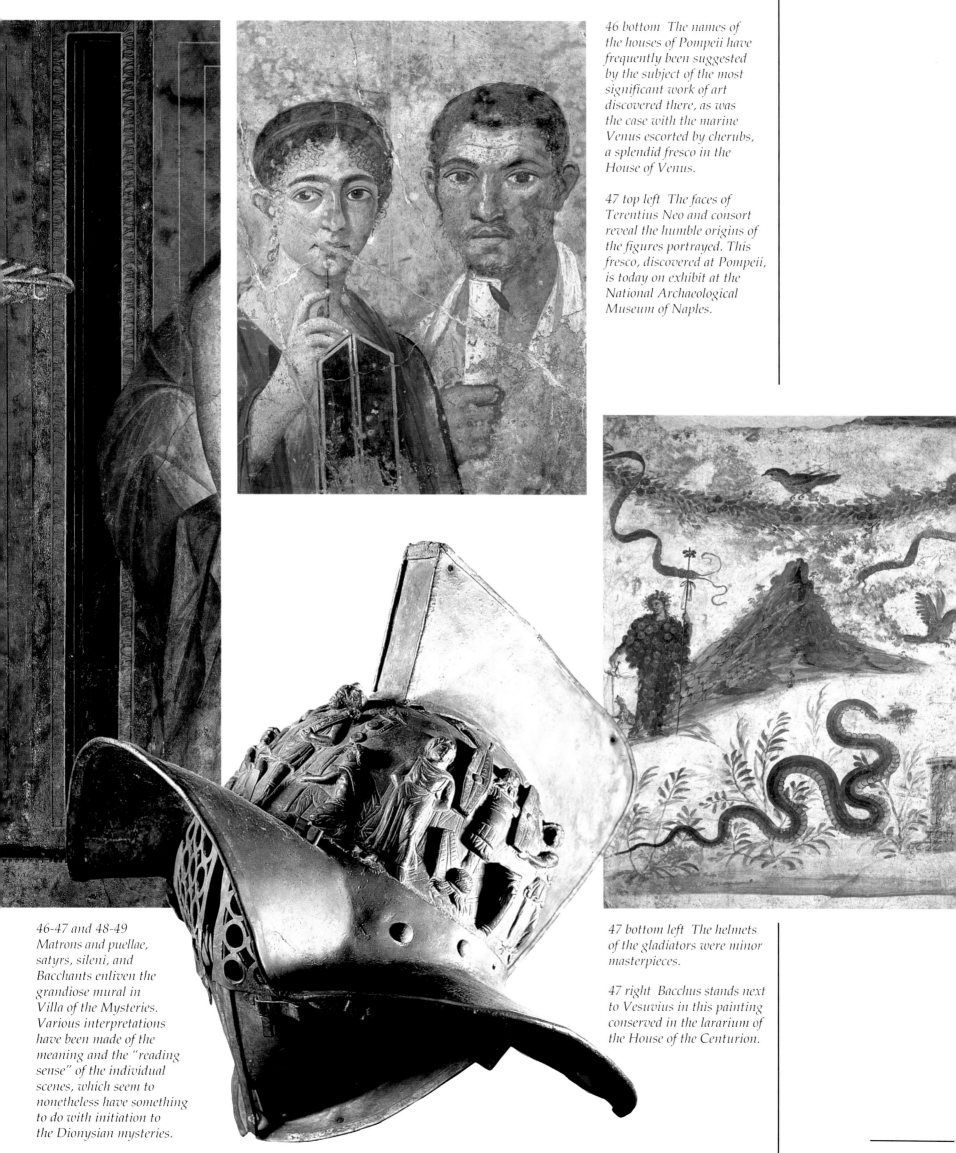

46 bottom The names of the houses of Pompeii have frequently been suggested by the subject of the most significant work of art discovered there, as was the case with the marine Venus escorted by cherubs, a splendid fresco in the House of Venus.

47 top left The faces of Terentius Neo and consort reveal the humble origins of the figures portrayed. This fresco, discovered at Pompeii, is today on exhibit at the National Archaeological Museum of Naples.

46-47 and 48-49 Matrons and puellae, satyrs, sileni, and Bacchants enliven the grandiose mural in Villa of the Mysteries. Various interpretations have been made of the meaning and the "reading sense" of the individual scenes, which seem to nonetheless have something to do with initiation to the Dionysian mysteries.

47 bottom left The helmets of the gladiators were minor masterpieces.

47 right Bacchus stands next to Vesuvius in this painting conserved in the lararium of the House of the Centurion.

47

their arms to the gods. A great many cried that the gods were no more, [and] that the night would be eternal, the last night of the world...

The treasures, the frescoes, the houses, along with everyday things such as bread, grain, the benches of the taverns, objects and mosaics, glimpses and scenes of life in the city of the rich and the city of the servants, the atmosphere of the market, the temples, the forum, the theaters, all were buried beneath a pall of stone, immortalized in the sleep of centuries, suspended and handed down, as if under a spell, to the time of the first

51 top The House of the Vettii is a treasure chest crammed with works of art. For example, the triclinia or dining room, with the typical vermilion that dominates the beautiful frescoes, is the house's most famous and most richly decorated room.

51 center The oecus, with decoration in yellow and red, was one of the main rooms of the House of the Vettii. Among the scenes painted on the walls of this room, of particular note is the one depicting Hercules as a child strangling the snakes and the one showing the Bacchants tearing Pentheus to pieces.

51 bottom The broad peristyle around the garden of the House of Vettii was completely frescoed. Today only traces of the pictorial work that decorated it can be seen.

archaeological excavations sixteen centuries later. The houses reappeared and along with them scenes of the drama. Liquid plaster was poured into the voids that bodies consumed by time had left behind in the pall of ashes. Thus re-emerged the body of a slave re-emerged who died with her arms above her head, clasping a roof tile used a shield to defended herself against the flood of fire. Another woman was discovered supine, while the chain that prevented its escape is still around a dog's neck. Fleeing figures were transformed into stone statues.

"Many disasters have happened in the world, but

50-51 The mosaic of the Strolling Players comes from the Villa of Cicero at Pompeii. This small work is an emblem constructed of minute tesserae.

50 bottom The domus of the wealthy merchants, Aulo Vettio Restituto and Aulo Vettio Conviva, the House of the Vettii was decorated with magnificent frescoes.

never has such delight been provided by such a grave tragedy. I believe it would be difficult to see anything else so interesting," commented Goethe on visiting the wonders of the buried cities, today famous throughout the world. The villas of Popea and Crassus at ancient Oplontis, now Torre Annunziata, have also been restored. The middle class residences of Herculaneum, were buildings composed of a number of floors with apartments overlooking a porticoed courtyard. There was the beautiful "Trellis House" and the hotel, with a terrace supported by vaults and extending towards the sea. A house with a mosaic-decorated atrium had beautiful panoramic gardens. There were the thermal baths, the gymnasium and sporting area, the sumptuous House of Deer, and thousand other marvels. A few miles away, two cities now converge. In modern Pompeii, a constant stream of pilgrims pay homage to the miraculous image on the altar of the shrine of the Madonna del Rosario, a tall campanile towering over a sea of houses. Next door, there is the great Roman Pompeii that once boasted thirty thousand inhabitants in an area of 163 acres. Interminable research continues to prize from the ground fragments that compile a mosaic of a wealthy and attractive city. Some of the world's most famous and fascinating archaeological digs have revived a city that can be explored with its regular grid of streets and rediscovered treasure by treasure. Among the artifacts are some of the most beautiful houses of the ancient civilization and those with the richest frescoes and mosaics. There is also the forum with the temple of Venus and the basilica where justice was administered and business concluded, the theaters and the amphitheater, the macellum where meat was butchered and sold, the domus, and the shops of Abundance Street, the Capitolium where Jupiter, Juno, and Minerva were venerated, the temple built at the behest of Silla in honor of Venus, and the palace of the priestess Eumakia. Beyond the city walls, there are the funerary monuments of Tomb Street and the Villa of the Mysteries, famous for its beautiful frescoes associated with the Dionysian cult.

52 A shaft of light between four columns illuminates the vestibule of the suburban thermal baths of ancient Herculaneum. Here too life was turned to stone by the erupting Vesuvius which covered the city with a mantle of mud and lava.

53 top and center The fantastic figure of a triton features in the mosaic that forms the floor of the changing room, the apodyterium, of the female section of the urban thermal baths at Herculaneum. The entrance to the male section (center) was on the other side of the complex. Each section was independent, each with its own series of rooms from the frigidarium to the tepidarium and the calidarium.

53 bottom The houses of present-day Ercolano have closed in on the excavations of Herculaneum, the city founded by Hercules, much of which still remains buried and inaccessible beneath the foundations of the modern buildings.

54 This statue of a Danaide was found in the Villa dei Papiri at Herculaneum. The Danaides were the mythical daughters of Danaus, condemned for killing their husbands to pour water into a bottomless pit for ever.

55 The athlete, is one of the bronze statues from the Villa dei Papiri, now exhibited in the National Archaeological Museum at Naples. Some ninety bronze or marble sculptures were found here, along with a collection of papyruses conserved in the National Library in Naples.

The collections of relics are magnificent. Frescoes and paintings, marble work, mosaics, precious bronzes, jewellery, and vases with exquisite decoration narrating exotic stories are on display. The masterpieces that once decorated the walls and floors of rich and elegant cities evoke the atmosphere of the time. Today they are kepted in the halls of the National Archaeological Museum of Naples, a treasure chest of the most significant works, some previously held in the Royal Palace at Portici. At King Charles of Bourbon's behest, the relics recovered by the first Bourbon excavators to explore the narrow tunnels of what was, a kind of archaeological mine among the walls of the ancient houses, were conserved there. The intriguing accounts of the first European aristocrats to complete the Grand Tour marked a turning point in the slow rediscovery of Pompeii and Herculaneum. This was in the eighteenth century, when the first ruins discovered inspired poetry, stories, and paintings, while Europe was gripped by the enthralling adventure of the excavations. In a two-thousand-year leap through time, the giant Vesuvius gave back a civilization and culture it had annihilated in an instant. At Pompeii the population did not even have the time to raise their eyes to the sky to invoke Venus Pompeiana, the patron goddess of the city who, dressed in blue with a golden aura, dispensed prosperity and good fortune. There are diverse theories to explain why the tragedy happened so quickly such as a cloud of incandescent vapor, or perhaps a rain of ashes as violent as an avalanche. Once the inferno passed, Herculaneum had disappeared beneath a sea of mud and of Pompeii all that could be seen were the highest roofs, those that 23 feet of ashes had failed to erase. Within a few years of the tragedy, the buried history and civilization had already been forgotten.

56-57 Hercules, the founder of Herculaneum according to legend, appears portrayed with the goddesses Minerva and Juno in a large fresco in the College of the Augustales.

56 bottom left Oplontis, on the slopes of Vesuvius, still conserves splendid frescoes that, along with statues, decorated the villas, and in terms of style and color resemble those of nearby Pompeii.

56 bottom right Villa Poppea at Oplontis had airy loggias and a large pool. At the moment of the eruption of 79 it was uninhabited, possibly due to damage caused during the earthquake of seventeen years earlier.

57 left An entrance portico welcomes visitors to the House of the Relief of Telephus at Herculaneum which takes its name from a magnificent marble bas-relief.

57 top right The mosaics and the frescos of the House of the Mosaic of Neptune and Amphitrite still retain surprisingly vivid colors and are characterized by the elegance of their compositions.

57 bottom right The rare beauty of the mosaic in which two deities are portrayed and which acted as a backdrop to the dining room, has made this ancient domus famous as the House of the Mosaic of Neptune and Amphitrite.

SEA AND HISTORY:
THE COAST OF THE SIRENS

Lemon and olive groves, rows of grape vines set
amid bare rock walls and ancient forests of oak and
chestnut grow, and on the hills majestic, centuries-old
pines rise proudly. Greenery and rock graze the waves,
steep cliffs rise from the sea, and a mosaic of colors are
reflected in the water before a range of mountains in the
background.

The landscape enchants. According to the ancient
legends, this was the land of the Sirens, women, with
the bodies of birds, messengers of Persephone the
goddess of the Underworld who seduced sailors with
sweet songs in order to steal their souls. Ulysses passed
this way. He resisted the Sirens by having himself
lashed to the mast of his ship so that he could hear the
music without surrendering to the flattery. "The sirens
seated in a beautiful meadow sing from shrewd lips to
entice travelers, but nearby a mountain of human bones,
putrefying corpses, and rotting skin rises," recounts
Homer's Odyssey. However, enchanted by the music of
Orpheus, they threw themselves into the sea and became
rocks: that seem black as the sun plunges into the sea at
dusk, coloring the horizon with a fiery red. They are

58-59 The bright green of the vegetation and the pallor of the dry rock plunge into the blue of the sea between Nerano and Positano. According to myths, it was here that the Sirens, enchanted by the music of Orpheus, threw themselves into the water and became rocks, known as the islands Li Galli.

59 top The rugged coastline offers no safe havens for the fishing boats of Priano. The old fishing villages along the two coasts that divide the Bay of Naples from that of Salerno are hemmed in by narrow, rocky inlets or cling to the rock walls that rise around minuscule bays.

known as Li Galli, isands that once belonged to l'etoile Nureyev, in the waters off Positano.

In this enchanted land, extending towards the island of Capri, closing the Bay of Naples to the north and to the south that of Sorrento. On one side lies the beauty of the Sorrentine coast and on the other the pearls of the Amalfitana coast. Further south, another tongue of rock pushes out into the open sea towards a small island with a lighthouse called Punta Licosa, the Promontory of the Sirens. The trees have bowed to the power of the winds blowing off the sea, bending towards the crown of gentle hills. The singing of the crickets covers the incessant beat of the waves striking the brow of rock where the deep blue of a transparent sea finishes and the lighter, livelier green of the forest of aleppo pines begins. This is the land of Leucothea, the beautiful temptress who sang while reclining on the rocks.

Once again the myth of the Siren's song is used to describe this coastline. The early travelers of ancient times found nothing more fitting than such fantasies to convey the rare beauty of places that left them breathless. This is the Cilento coast, rugged and tattered along a series of promontories covered with olive groves, tiny bays that surrender themselves to the sea, and golden beaches at the foot of dense pine forests.

From Naples southwards, the Sorrentine, Amalfitana, and Cilento coasts present common traits that reveal their secrets. They are isolated on the sea by the mountains, traversed by narrow roads that wind in a seemingly endless sequence of hairpin turns, with sheer drops to one side and bare rock walls to the other. Their villages are fishing communities, today among the pearls of Italian tourism, that have never shed the signs of simple lives based on sacrifice and labor. In this land of sailors of the Mediterranean routes and beyond, there are traces of encounters with distant cultures, evidence of the Orient, and the influence of Arabs. It is also a land of farmers who, over the centuries, have striven to reclaim patches of land from the harshness of the landscape, succeeding in the apparently impossible task of creating narrow terraces of tillable earth where once there was nothing but woods and rock, in precarious equilibrium on precipitous slopes, with patience and effort raising muracine, low walls of stone and mud. The crops climbing over hills that plunge into the sea are a thing of wonder. This is the first image that strikes the traveler, as the road constructed at the behest of Ferdinand of Bourbon in 1834 heads towards Punta Campanella after having skirted around Vesuvius. It is a landscape of dramatic contrasts: the yellow of the lemons, in long rows beneath the pergolas that offer them shelter from the burning sun, the silver of the olive trees, amid the fine black nets that at summer's end are used for the harvest, the intense green of the vines, and the yellow flowering broom. Varying tones can be dull in the areas of grass burnt by the sun, but shine bright in the patches of luxuriant trees. Myriad colors are reflected in the deep blue of the sea and the sea is overlooked by tiny villages with intricate staircases and alleys designed to thwart marauders from the sea.

60-61 The pines at Punta Licosa, which in ancient times was known as the Promontory of the Sirens, almost dip their roots in the sea. Legend has it that the siren Leucosia threw herself from the rocks and was buried on this tongue of land.

61 bottom The lighthouse on the little island of Licosa rises alongside the stones of ancient walls. These are the remains of a city of the past buried by the sea, the waters of which conceal the porticoes and floors of magnificent villas.

62 top From the splendid
terraces of Sorrento
overlooking the sea towards
the Bay of Naples, one can
admire the celebrated views
characterized by the
unmistakable shape of
Vesuvius.

62 bottom Among the few
accessible points of the craggy
Sorrentine coast, of particular
note is the beach at Alimuri.

Vico Equense, Meta, and then the elegant
Sorrento are set upon a great block of tuff emerging
from the sea. Sorrento, with its noble and ancient
history, is today a favorite destination for
international tourism. Surrentum was the Greek
city of the Sirens. It became a favorite of the Roman
aristocracy who, following the example set by
Tiberius who had chosen for himself the hills of the
neighboring island of Capri, built majestic villas
here for their vacations by the sea. Kitchen and
ornamental gardens providing lemons, oranges, and
grapes used to make wine have always been a feature
of the area. Walnuts and lemons, in old, simple
recipes, lend flavor to strong, aromatic liqueurs.
Nocillo and limoncello have become ever-present
after meals are such symbols of this land that both
Sorrento and nearby Capri have laid rival claims to
its paternity. The center of Sorrento is a suggestive
maze of narrow streets and shops. Skilled craftsmen
hand down the secrets of ancient traditions for
making laces, silks, and the incredible parquetry that
uses thousands of different colored tiny fragments
of wood to trace images that seem painted.

The coasts runs straight from here until the
Promontorium Minervae, as the ancient Romans
named Punta della Campanella. Built in the
fourteenth century, Torre di Minerva, high above
the two bays, rang a bell that would echo from
village to village and raise the alarm when the
silhouette of a pirate ship appeared above the
horizon, bringing with it the threat of attacks, raids,
and nights of terror. Today, the ruined tower extends
an imaginary hand toward the island of Capri.

62-63 The green of the
Belvedere in front of the
Museo Correale di Terranova
at Sorrento overlooks the
small port of Marina Piccola.
The fishing boats are drawn
up on the little village's
beach, safe from the
inhospitable sea, while the
city behind extends on
terraces high above the sea.

63 bottom left Barely visible
among the narrow streets
tracing the path of the
ancient cardus and
decumanus of Roman
Sorrento, the bell-tower of
the Duomo of Sorrento rises
above an arch with four
ancient recycled columns. At
the top, the lovely ceramic
clock was locally made.

63 bottom right Older
people love to meet and play
cards in the old quarter of
Sorrento, sitting at tables
under the fifteenth century
frescoes of the Sedile
Dominova. This is the
ancient home of one of the
four sedili, or seats, into
which the city nobles were
once divided.

An oasis of elite tourism, Capri has been a location for aristocratic vacations ever since the dawn of its history. It proudly recalls the imperial vacations of Augustus and Tiberius who decided to remain here until his death. Today the visitors are known as VIPs and still regularly return to crowd the streets of the medieval quarter with shops selling the leather sandals made by the local craftsmen alongside clothes bearing the most fashionable of labels. There are obligatory stops for a coffee or a granita at the tables in the celebrated piazzetta between the small church of Santo Stefano and the tower with the famous clock in majolica. Among sophisticated cafes and luxurious hotels, as well as trattorias and modest workshops, there is a marriage between an international atmosphere and local tradition, within the frame of a surreal landscape and a sea of dreams.

The island is a limestone block bathed by the rays of the sun whose delicately reflecting tones inspired the nickname Isola Azzurra (Blue Island). The landscape is rugged with towering crags of rock. A natural arch rises on the east coast. Below the Tragara viewpoint, three stacks soar: Stella, attached to the coast at 358 feet, Scopolo at 341 feet, and the smallest at 266 feet, the last two home to nesting gulls. On the summit of these rocks surrounded by the sea and nowhere else, the rare blue lizard has chosen to live and survive.

The rocky coastline continues in a complex sequence of highs and lows. There are many caves,

64 top From the vacations of the emperor Tiberius to those of the modern-day VIPs, Capri has never lost its position as one of the pearls of national and international tourism. Alongside the villas and the great hotels, however, remains the simple appeal of streets and white houses contrasting with the intense color of the sea and the blue reflections on the living rock.

64 bottom The rays of the sun enter via a great opening on the sea floor and, as if by magic, diffuse a blue light so intense as to render the great Grotta Azzurra one of the world's most famous natural spectacles.

64-65 High rock walls rise behind the port of Marina Grande, where large wooden boats await tourists taking

excursions to the Grotta Azzurra or a tour around the island of Capri in search of the most suggestive corners of an enchanting coast.

65 bottom Rugged pinnacles of rock, the Faraglioni rise powerfully from the bottom of a deep blue sea. The coast of Capri is composed of high, inaccessible cliffs and patches of green.

small hollows, and great halls. In all 65 caverns open onto the sea. The queen, the celebrated Grotta Azzurra, has just a small opening onto the sea and is entered by crouching in small wooden boats. Inside, it is broad and majestic, the light filtering from below creating a unique deep blue atmosphere.

Capri offers promenades along the sea front, terraces, the Augusto park and the Cannone viewpoint, Via Krupp, constructed at the behest of the German industrialist whose name it bears which rises from the sea, climbing in a series of tight hairpin

66 top left A minor work of art but of exquisite beauty, the square in Capri is as famous throughout the world as the people who frequent it.

66 top right Mount Solaro dominates the bright white houses of Capri, one of the island's two communes. Anacapri, instead, is found higher up, immersed in greenery.

turns up a rocky spur, the choir of the fourteenth century Certosa di San Giacomo, and further up at Anacapri (the second largest commune on the island), the terraces of Villa San Michele and the Belvedere di Migliara. Still higher are the woods of Mount Solaro. Every garden, every villa, every terrace provides spectacular views of a rare beauty from compositions of rock and sea, to the Bay of Naples from Cape Miseno, to the sovereign Sant'Agata dei due Golfi overlooking the sea on either side of the tip of Punta della Campanella.

66 bottom right Punta di Capo appears to leap powerfully from the sea. From above, Capri seems a huge rock marking the southernmost tip of the Bay of Naples.

66-67 No one uses the official name of Piazza Umberto I as it is now universally known

simply as "la piazzetta," a symbol of Capri, its open air café tables a chic setting for a rendezvous.

67 bottom left The southern coast of Capri is a vertical rock wall rising directly from the sea, touched only by the few houses of Marina Piccola.

67 bottom right Steep cliffs form a barrier between Capri and its sea. Challenging this hostile morphology, the German industrialist Krupp had a road, which now bears his name, built to reach Marina Piccola.

68 top White houses, piled one on top of the other in a labyrinth of streets and steps, create a suggestive spectacle on the cliffs that to the north enclose Amalfi. The ancient town is set in a narrow gorge rising from the sea.

Further to the east the Amalfitana coast opens into the Bay of Salerno, winding from one noble town to the next along ravines, crags, rock pinnacles, and terraces. Deep gorges cut into the hills and descend swiftly towards the rocks, tiny beaches, villages of white houses clinging to the rock, lanes, and steps leading up from the shore, winding around attractive churches that, overlooking the sea, accompanied the ships of sailors and fishermen who set sail in search of fortune. Amalfi was once nothing but a tiny village locked in a rocky cove with no streets, just an opening onto the infinity of the sea. It went on to become a powerful Maritime Republic in the same league as Genoa, Venice, and Pisa, its ships dominating the world. Departing from that village isolated by high mountains, their vessels encountered distant cultures and returned to transform their humble community into an ever richer and more beautiful town. The elegant Amalfi still bears the mark of journeys to Tunis, Alexandria, and Constantinople, but conserves its local customs, and protects an agricultural and craft tradition it has never forsaken. The historic Albergo dei Cappucini, set on a cliff above the sea below a rocky backdrop, with its thirteenth century cloister and attractive garden that appears to be suspended in the void, offers the most beautiful view. Amalfi boasts a beautiful sea-front, the variously colored marble of the Duomo dominating the piazza from the top of a colossal flight of steps, the campanile with its thousand-year history standing alongside, and the extraordinarily beautiful Chiostro del Paradiso, built in the thirteenth century as a worthy cemetery for the most illustrious citizens. In the town there are yet more steep steps and narrow lanes, climbing the narrow gully of the Valle dei Mulini that slips between high green and rocky wings where the water of small streams once powered the old paper mills. The ancient art of handmade paper still survives, a unique product known and appreciated throughout the world under the brand name Carta di Amalfi.

The tight curves of the nineteenth century coast road, cut into the rock, and the long pass through Chiunzi through the Lattari mountains are the only roads communicating with the Amalfitana coast.

Crowded if not overwhelmed by a florid tourist industry increasingly characterized by the long vacations of VIPs (queens and princesses, sheikhs and heads of state have all stayed here in recent years), the area remains a treasure chest jealously conserving ancient jewels.

68 center Between Capo d'Orso and Capo di Conca, and further on as far as the Punta di Priano, the coast on either side of Amalfi is a sequence of rocky peaks in daring equilibrium above the sea.

68 bottom Fiordo di Furore is a tiny fishing village nestled in a narrow crack in the rock high above the sea. Composed of a series of cottages clinging to the steep slopes, it overlooks a thin strip of sand on which the boats are pulled up.

68-69 A play of light evidences, in strong contrast with the dark sea, the point that to the south of the old town culminates in the Torre di Amalfi. From this point, look-outs once scanned the horizon to gave warning of approaching enemy ships.

69 bottom The famous
Duomo in Amalfi is
dedicated to St. Andrew.
It dominates the square
from the top of a long, steep
stairway which further
accentuates the liveliness of
the forms and colors of the
façade. Note the sheets of gold
foil that shine in the sunlight.

70-71 The golden rays of the
sun at dusk reflect off the sea
and bathe the coast of Amalfi.

This is a landscape that
enchants even in winter, with
the dark sky, the few white
houses below the rocks, and
the fishing boats on the water.

72-73 White comets of foam
are created by dozens of
yachts and leisure boats along
a tract of the Amalfi Coast.

74-75 Farming terraces
descend precipitously along a
slope near Ravello.

76 top The lanes of Positano conceal features with an eastern flavor. Palms and banana trees are the heritage of a population of navigators who reached distant lands, while in the courtyards there is a riot of color with the brilliant hibiscus and the various tints of the bougainvillea.

Large, small, or even tiny, towns, villages, and minuscule fishing communities like Fiordo di Furore have grown in the ravines carved into the coastline by the waters of the torrents, protected to the rear by the mountains and offering the narrowest and most easily defensible of apertures against raiders from the sea. Furore is nothing more than a minute fishing village, with a suggestive cluster of houses clambering one on top of another in an impossibly narrow gorge and apparently carved directly from the living rock. Cottages such as those that at Praiano climb up the slopes of Mount Sant'Angelo and around the church of San Luca, in order to overlook the enchanting marina at Praia. To the west is the stunning Grotta dello Smeraldo, a sea cave containing remarkable green reflections. Yet another beautiful church and yet another labyrinth of lanes in the valley that between Punta Germano and Cape Sottile descends to the sea can be found in the much sought after area, Positano, also distinguished by a rather elite form of tourism. Palm trees grow in the gardens between the white houses with their rounded, Oriental-style roofs, and a maze of lanes surround the majolica-decorated church of Santa Maria Assunta. Numerous artists' workshops are located here. The art of cotton design with characteristic patterns and colors enlivens the streets with a rainbow of a thousand scarves, light dresses flapping in the wind like flags, and the famous swimming costumes. The large beach comes right up to the houses, with the parade of wooden fishing boats pulled up out of the water alongside one another.

Further along there are many other smaller beaches, a sequence of little bays enclosed and defended by a frame of greenery and rock. Some of them are deserted or almost inaccessible except by way of long flights of steps and narrow footpaths, secret routes which those in the know never reveal for fear that their tiny, secluded sport may be transformed into a patch of sand crowded with deckchairs and sunshades.

A little higher up, as if by magic, Ravello presents the spell of music that accompanies the setting sun or the first pink rays of dawn. The concerts of Villa Rufolo, frequently held at unusual times in order to capture the most suggestive moments in an incomparable natural setting, are among the most prestigious events of the Amalfitana coast's cultural calendar. The panorama behind the stage suspended over the sea, with the blue stretching out just beyond the dome of the thirteenth century church of the Annunciation, in a setting of exotic plants, is itself a spectacle, a sight that inspired Wagner's garden of Klingsor in the second act of Parsifal. In the thirteenth century the Rufolo family decided to built an attractive Byzantine-style villa here.

Ravello was then a rich trading town on the routes to the Orient and it still retains Arabic and Asian influences of rare elegance.

76 center From the beach enclosed by cliffs, Positano climbs upwards in a maze of steps and narrow streets that snake between the white-painted houses.

76 bottom From the town of Positano that gently slopes into the sea, the Amalfitano coast runs south through numerous tiny promontories such as the point at Paiano.

76-77 The imposing majolica-decorated dome of the parish church dedicated to Our Lady of the Assumption watches over the fishing boats pulled up onto the beach and dominates the houses of the old center of Positano.

77 bottom A canopy of canes protects a belvedere in Positano from the sun, the immaculate balustrade setting off the colors of the geraniums. The belvederes overlooking enchanting views are a recurrent architectural feature of the most prestigious houses on the Amalfitana coast.

79 top On the narrow beach of Praiano, sunbathers crowd in next to the fishermen's boats in dry dock.

79 bottom Camellias, begonias, hydrangeas, and geraniums surround the two towers of Villa Cimbrone, in Ravello, famous for the view from its belvedere.

80-81 The houses and streets of Positano, like contour lines on a map, faithfully follow the conformation of the territory.

82-83 A human-sized nativity scene, one typical to Campania, announces the village of Atrani, near Amalfi and a participant in Amalfi's ancient glory days.

78-79 The colors of the majolica decorating the dome and the campanile of the church of San Gennaro stand out in clear contrast to the dark blue of the sea at Vettica Maggiore, a short distance from Praiano.

78 bottom left The elegance of a centuries-old pine dominates a panorama that arouses strong emotions. Here, the bay

at Maiori is seen from the terraces of the ancient Villa Rufolo at Ravello.

78 bottom right An unusual Arab-Sicilian style can be seen in the noble palaces of Ravello, celebrated for its enchanting flower gardens. Tradition has it that the town was founded in the 6th century during the second Gothic war.

84-85 A patchwork of greenery and dry calcareous cliffs falls steeply from the top of the Latteri mountains. Vietri sul Mare is the first town that one encounters heading south along the winding Amalfitana coast road.

84 bottom Rock sculpted into the most fantastic shapes plunges for 656 feet into the sea along the Amalfitana coast. Capo d'Orso separated the bay of Maiori from that of Vietri sul Mare. In front of the old look-out tower, the ships of Filippo Doria defeated Charles V's fleet in 1528.

85 top Myriad workshops with brilliant colors perpetuate an ancient craft tradition. The hand-painted ceramics of Vietri sul Mare, famous throughout the world, feature unique decoration.

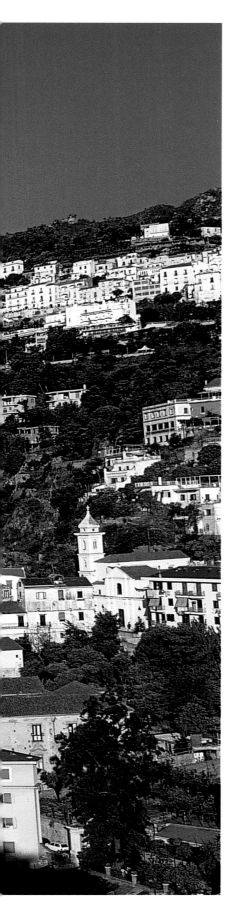

The colors of the sea and the environment, the lemons, and the grapes can be seen in the lively ceramic decorations of Vietri sul Mare, minor masterpieces of a craft with deeply rooted traditions. The streets are invaded by the stalls of a hundred workshops, tiny enterprises where works so attractive and so fragile are piled incredibly high, one on top of another, filling all available space. To make your way through this labyrinth of wonders and discover and choose the most beautiful motifs and objects requires care and patience. Coffee cups and trays, carafes, bottles, amphorae and large vases, fabulous plates, tables combining ceramics with wrought iron, and heavy tiles as attractive as the extremely old and valuable ones that glitter on the dome of the eighteenth church dedicated to Saint John the Baptist are for sale.

Feelings and religious tradition have also been linked through history to the isolation imposed by such a rugged landscape. Each parish has its own church, its patron saint to hear the prayers of those who have entrusted their destiny to the sea, and the hugely popular rituals of thanksgiving processions. The monks, in a long distant past, retreated into the narrowest ravines, little more than niches, and quarried the stone they needed to build churches and monasteries that appear suspended on the rocks.

At Maiori, the suggestive and venerable abbey of Santa Maria de Olearia is perched among the olive trees. It contains frescoed walls, the narrow cells of the monks later transformed into the urns of the abbey's catacomb, and three superimposed chapels. Inland from the coast, beyond the first hills dominating the sea, set amid sheer rock walls and the green of Mount Finestra, is the thousand-year-old Benedictine abbey of the Holy Trinity. The beautiful building holds precious treasures, books, and works of art. The original medieval community of the noble Cava dei Tirreni is at Corpo di Cava, a town that boasts porticoed streets in the ancient Borgo Scacciaventi and a setting of gentle hills painted a thousand times by the celebrated landscape artists of the Posillipo school. With discreet elegance and a style very different to that of many other towns of the region that have grown too rapidly in an unplanned explosion of concrete, Cava passionately conserves medieval traditions that have disappeared elsewhere: costumed processions, flag twirlers famous throughout the world, and the pistone or the medieval harquebus, jealously conserved by the head of each family who hands down the art of loading and shooting it. The explosions echo in the great costumed reconstructions held at the Festival of Montecastello and the Challenge for the White Parchment.

85 center Only the narrow curtain of the Lattari Mountains separates the Cava dei Tirreni, which has preserved the charm of when, in the 1800s, it was a typical stop for travelers on the Grand Tour, from the sea.

85 bottom At Cava dei Tirreni each year the earth shakes with the rumbling of the ancient "pistoni" being fired. During three days of celebrations, over a thousand costumed figures re-evoke first the great terror and then the defeat of the plague of 1656.

86-87 Luxuriant cultivated areas extend along the Amalfi Coast, protected by the mountains from the colder northern weather patterns.

88-89 and 88 bottom
The Sanctuary of Athena,
also known as the Temple of
Ceres, dates back to the dawn
of the Ancient Greek colony
of Poseidonia.

89 top The area of the
Forum, in Paestum, was
a large rectangular town
square of 492 by 187 feet,
encircled by a portico on
at least three sides.

89 bottom The Temple of
Neptune, built around the
middle of the fifth century
B.C., has a powerful
structure and perfect
proportions.

90-91 The orderly layout of
a part of the ancient colony
is still clearly visible in this
view of Paestum, centered on
the Basilica and the Temple
of Neptune.

Some miles further south, on the wide Bay of
Salerno, the temples of Paestum are the gateway to
the Cilento, evidence of ancient Poseidonia, a rich
colony of Ancient Greece founded six centuries before
Christ on the banks of the river Sele. They stand
majestic, evocative at dusk silhoutted against the
setting sun filtering between the towering columns
and the massive architraves. The Via Sacra passes by
the so-called Basilica dedicated to the goddess Hera,
revered by the Achaei, the Temple of Neptune, and
the Temple of Athena, as it crosses the Greek agora
and the Roman forum. Outside the walls of the
ancient city, at the mouth of the river Sele, little
remains of the beautiful, imposing sanctuary that
Jason had built as a worthy tribute to Hera Argiva,
a symbol of solidarity between the peoples of diverse
extraction who founded colonies in southern Italy.
The complex included a huge temple and smaller
votive chapels, as every town and city in Ancient
Greece built to honor the gods that protected them.

92-93 *The Lucanian tombs, such as the sarcophagus with a pitched top seen here, have conserved paintings of rare beauty to the present day. The Lucanians occupied the area of the Greek colony of Poseidonia before the Romans founded Paestum.*

92 bottom left *Painted on the cover of the tomb that takes its name, the scene of 'the Diver" is the most famous of the decorations discovered in the Greek necropolises of the Poseidonia area.*

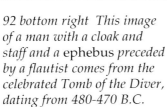

92 bottom right *This image of a man with a cloak and staff and a* ephebus *preceded by a flautist comes from the celebrated Tomb of the Diver, dating from 480-470 B.C.*

93 top *A fragment of a fresco, exhibited in the Museum of Paestum, conserves the elegant representation of a figure on horseback. The museum houses numerous interesting relics found in the painted tombs of the area and other parts of the Cilento coast.*

93 bottom *A banquet scene adorns one of the sides of the so-called Tomb of the Diver found in the Paestum area. These paintings are unique in that among the relics of the colonies of Ancient Greece, there are no other examples of figurative art.*

94-95 This suggestive aerial view of the Certosa of San Lorenzo at Padula reveals its impressive size. Built on an area of over 538,200 square feet, it is considered to be one of the most important historic buildings in southern Italy.

94 bottom The houses at Padula peek from behind the elegant internal facade overlooking the cloister of the Certosa of San Lorenzo. The imposing building was erected in 1306 by Tommaso Sanseverino, Count of Marsico.

From this point, the province of Salerno, the most extensive in Campania, slips southwards as far as that thin strip of Lucania from which Maratea overlooks the Tyrrhenian, but a stone's throw from Calabria.

In the shaping of the Alburni mountains at Pertosa in the heart of hills overlooking the valley of the river Tanagro, a subterranean stream carved the spectacle of the so-called Caverns of the Angel, or of St. Michael, into the rock sculpting gorges and tunnels of great mystery, with stalactites reflected in the water, waterfalls, and springs. The river below the ground was once inhabited, as demonstrated by the Neolithic pileworks and traces of a mysterious cult practiced up to a thousand years ago. During the same period, a few miles to the south at Padula, at the foot of Mount Maddalena, the first medieval walls of the monastery, constructed at the behest of Count Sanseverino, a nephew of St. Thomas Aquinas, were raised and continued to grow ever larger and more beautiful over the centuries. Dedicated to San Lorenzo, a masterpiece of art, a center of economic wealth, and famous as a haven of culture, it was also renowned for the great hospitality of its monks. Stories are still told about the incredible thousand-egg omelette prepared for Charles V and his entire retinue.

The 129,000 square feet cloister is one of the world's largest. Built along lines that seem to interlock like those of a chessboard, it recalls the gridiron of the martyrdom of St. Lawrence. One particular curiosity is the permanent exhibition dedicated to Joe Petrosino, the celebrated Italo-American policeman, a son of these lands, assassinated at Palermo in 1906.

High mountains dominate the valley. Six peaks over of 5577 feet constitute the Alburni range, including Mounts Sacro, Cervati and Motola. Amid woods and gorges, deep scars have been dug by the Calore and Sammaro rivers, the torrents running between high walls of calcareous rock, and caves and springs abound.

Tiny clusters of houses defend an agricultural heritage based on real labor and real passion, authentic flavors, and simple yet sincere values. The landscape, in suggestive synthesis, marries with the sea, from Agropoli towards Punta Licosa, and south towards Cape Palinuro. This is a melting pot of diverse realities and atmospheres, with the unique appeal of the Cilento National Park and the Vallo di Diano.

An ancient Byzantine acropolis, Agropoli features old houses lining the former maritime center's port.

95 top The woods of the Cilento region, a stone's throw from an enchanting sea, jealously defend the heritage of a rich agricultural tradition. The Cilento National park boasts unspoiled and dramatically beautiful landscapes.

95 bottom The River Mingardo snakes for 25 miles through the heart of Cilento Park, amid rocks and woods, before flowing into the Bay of Policastro.

96 top The houses of the old center of Agropoli are reflected from a high promontory, set amid the rock and silvery olive trees, in the limpid Cilento sea.

Piers, Roman ships, amphorae and anchors, and tombs and columns are scattered in the sea of the four parishes of the mediaeval fortress of Castellabate that dominates from above the coast of Punta Licosa. The waves almost break on the doorsteps of Santa Maria's ancient houses, San Marco is a small port constructed alongside the original Greek and Roman piers, and beyond the point Ogliastro was born to satisfy the strong demand of seaside tourism. The stone houses built on the rocks at Acciaroli enchanted Ernest Hemingway. He spent much time there, and wrote about the appeal of the village and its minuscule port, about the colors of the mountain reflected in the sea, and about the golden beaches. At Velia (the Greek Elea), there are traces of a remote past. Founded by the Greeks and colonized by the Romans, the town was a major landing place, an important point of reference for the colonies of Ancient Greece, and celebrated for the philosophical school of Parmenides and Zeno that lent it prestige throughout the ancient world. The ruins of the Acropolis, the temple, and the theater still survive.

The coast around the port that bears the name of Palinuro, Anaeas' helmsman who fell into the sea here and died, once again has begun to experiment with bizarre, extravagant, and daring architecture. It is an enchanted curtain of harsh rocks that rise from the sea to recount fantastic stories. There is the cavern with its stalactites that turns blue at sunset, and dozens of other sea caves such as Cala del Ribalto, Cala del Salvatore, below the towering Punta Spartivento, and Cala della Lanterna. Sulphurous water gushes in the ravines of Cala Fetente. The Visco and Ciavole caves were inhabited in prehistoric times. In the Grotta delle Ossa, among the stalactites and stalagmites, appears a stunning mosaic of human and animal bones set in the walls. However, investigations by historians suggest much more distant origins.

A short distance down the coast at the river Mingardo, rises a spectacular natural arch.

96 center The walls and a gate at Velia are testimony to an ancient history. The town was founded by exiles from the city of Focea, fleeing from Asia Minor after the arrival of the Persians.

96 bottom The Porta Rosa of ancient Velia was for centuries a natural access route to the acropolis. It was not fortified until a thousand years after the foundation of the town in the fourth century B.C. by the Romans.

96-97 The lace-like coast conceals bays and caverns in the setting that saw the pilot of Aeneas, afflicted with deep sleep by Juno, fall into the sea and drown. According to the myth, Sybil had promised him that the site, the Promontory of Palinuro, would have taken his name.

97 bottom left The greenery of the Cilento acts as a frame for the intense color of the sea around the port of Palinuro. The economy of the tiny village, now discovered by tourism, was traditionally based on fishing.

97 bottom right At the mouth of the Mingardo, the natural arch is one of the wonders of the coast of the Promontory of Palinuro.

98-99 Rocks that push out
into the open sea enclose the
strip of sand of Cala Bianca
at Marina di Camerota in a
small and protected niche.
This wild and unspoiled
paradise invites one to search
out the jewels far from the
usual tourist routes.

98 bottom Tongues of eroded
rock in a series of caves and
ancient towers that once kept
vigil over the sea characterize
the cliffs of Marina di
Camerota, one of the most
attractive stretches of the
Cilento coast.

The coast winds its way between old villages and new temples of seaside tourism: the small town of Pioppi, Ascea, Pisciotta, and further south, Marina di Camerota, Scario, and Sapri on the remotest tip of Campania.

With so much history, the traces of the oldest colonies reappear in village after village. Greeks and Romans lived in a land that once belonged to the Lucanians. With the onset of the Middle Ages, the counties of the Longobard kingdom, grew richer and power struggles between the barons and the church increased. And today although uncontrolled for years, the disrespectful concrete and expanding tourism that threaten villages and history, has nonetheless failed to suffocate the appeal of a rich past and the natural beauty of the mountains the plunge into the sea.

99 top Rocks that seem to play with the sea offer enchanting views and an exceptional setting for the fishing village of Marina di Camerota.

99 bottom The Cilento coast seen from above shows all the unique appeal of an area adorned with woods that seem to rush to meet the waves and marked by rocks that trace the complex coastline.

NAPLES:
A MAGNIFICENT JEWEL BOX

100 top The fortress of Castel Sant'Elmo stands out high above the monumental center of Naples, with the Royal Palace and the Maschio Angioino that appears to be floating on the sea at the Molo Beverello.

100 center The glass skyscrapers of the business district tower over the old palaces, behind which Vesuvius keeps watch over both old Naples and the city of the future.

100 bottom Piazza Municipio, whic h opens in the heart of nineteenth century Naples, is still today the administrative center and a quarter crowded with offices.

Naples gazes at you with the bright eyes of a scugnizzo (a Neapolitan ragamuffin) kicking a football or sometimes timidly, with the fleeting glance of a woman hanging colorful washing on lines strung from window to window across the strip of sky seen from the narrow streets. The city shows the humble face of the popular quarters where daily life is bustling, authentic, sincere, and spontaneous, even though making ends meet might be truly difficult. Yet, it is also elegant, with the classic appeal of old squares, imposing castles, noble palazzi and evocative monasteries, cloisters, and churches. It is enchanting as it stretches out along the shoreline in the dazzling southern sun.

It is alive, with its own irrepressible intellectual fervor. A modern metropolis of the third millennium with glass towers soaring into the sky, the new city, the business district, is a futuristic quarter of skyscrapers designed by Kenzo Tange. As Naples rushes headlong into the future, it never forgets to pause and look back from time to time. It is a city capable of enchanting with a thousand stories handed down from generation to generation over the centuries. Listening to them can magically transform the atmosphere of places, quarters, works of art, and monuments that would otherwise be simply beautiful. Thanks to this tradition of story-telling, they become incredibly close and alive, cloaked in an atmosphere that is not abstract fantasy but rather intimately entwined with everyday life.

Every stone has a story. Every stone is bound to the lives of people who, over the centuries, have suffered without ever surrendering, have struggled without ever foregoing their innate joie de vivre.

101 top The elegant palaces of Via Partenope are reflected beyond the white stones of the breakwater in the Bay of Naples.

100-101 *On either side of the steps up to the stock exchange building dating from 1895, are two large bronze statuary groups. The building stands in the central Piazza Bovio where there is also a station of the new metropolitan railway line.*

102-103 *The skyscrapers of the Executive Center, the work of Kenzo Tange, stand out from the urban fabric of Naples.*

104-105 The liquefaction of the blood of the martyr San Gennaro, conserved in a sealed vial, is verified twice a year and for the Neapolitans the miracle is an auspicious sign.

104 bottom In the Duomo of Naples, the faithful, immersed in an atmosphere of participation, await in prayer for the execution of the miracle of San Gennaro.

Every monument has a story entwined with that of a street or a quarter with all its everyday events and its simple protagonists. There is the bancolotto where the numbers of the smorfia lottery have long been interpreted, the street seller marching back and forth hawking horns and charms to ward off bad luck, Pulcinella the clown who approaches playing a mandolin to ask for loose change, as well as the last of the posteggiatori, or car parkers, who sing the most beautiful of the traditional songs alongside the restaurant tables. Naples is also found in pizza eaten folded in four while standing in the street, in the oldest pizzerias where the service is basic and the authentic flavors and atmosphere are those of bygone times, in a delicious sfogliatella fresh from an antique oven, or in a soft babà soaked in rum. Strolling through the side-streets there is the old lady selling pieces of warm bread, the old man sitting on the front step of a basso, and the barman who, while preparing impeccable strong coffee, will fill one's head with chatter. Neapolitans love this chatter, they love to talk about their city and their lives from the significant to the banal.

Life blends with ancient rituals: the cults of the saints and the stories of princes and popular leaders evoke the eternal fracture between the lives of the ordinary people and those of the aristocracy.

Much more than a patron saint, San Gennaro is a friend when in need, one ready to lend an ear to accounts of everyday problems and the invocations of an entire city. In 1527, when Naples was terrorized by and powerless in the face of raging plague, a desperate plea was made, "San Gennaro, only you can stop it." In homage to the saint, Naples dedicated the opulent Treasury Chapel to him, a Baroque masterpiece in the great Duomo that Charles I d'Angiò commissioned in the late thirteenth century, transforming the early Christian basilica of Santa Restituta, built by the emperor Constantine 800 years earlier, into a side chapel. The miracle of the liquefaction of the saint's blood is repeated on the first Sunday in May and on the nineteenth of September, in a ritual dating back seven hundred years. The Neapolitans crowd into the church and the surrounding streets where the emotion and the tension, prayers and impatient expectation are palpable. The liquefaction is an auspicious occurrence and the city believes that if the saint does not perform the miracle serious calamities and suffering are on the horizon.

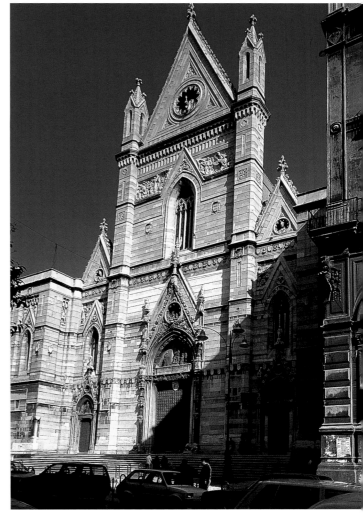

105 top The Duomo of Naples, inaugurated by Roberto d'Angiò in 1313, stands on the site previously occupied by two older basilicas, that of Santa Restituta from the fourth century, and that of Santa Stefania from the fifth. Remodeling, restorations, and earthquakes have over time modified the original appearance of the great cathedral.

105 bottom The church of the Madonna del Carmine, honored by the Neapolitans with a great feast day on July 16, also houses other images particularly dear to the local faithful: the Madonna Bruna and the wooden figure of the crucified Christ who, according to local tradition, bent his head to avoid a cannonball.

106 top A monumental door, on the top of which stands the bust of the saint, gives access from the nave of the cathedral to the Chapel of the Treasure of San Gennaro.

106 bottom A detail of the silver decoration of the altar, just one of the small part of the precious mosaic of works of art in the incredibly rich Chapel of the Treasure of San Gennaro.

106-107 The sumptuous Chapel of the Treasure of San Gennaro was built as a result of the vow the Neapolitan people made to their patron saint in return for his saving of the city from the plague of sixteenth century. Erected in the seventeenth century, it is a true masterpiece of Neapolitan Baroque, crowned by a large, fully frescoed dome.

On lunedí in Albis, or Monday in Albis, an army of twenty-five thousand faithful Catholics march from every quarter of the city, some on foot, others on their knees, sill others crawling with their faces to the ground, mile after mile towards the Sanctuary of Sant'Anastasia on the slopes of Vesuvius, as an offer to the Madonna dell'Arco. An ancient veiled cross is venerated in the Church of the Carmine, scene of the slaying of Masaniello whose speech to the people in the great market square sparked the rebellion of July 7, 1647. During the siege of the city by Alfonso of Aragon who was claiming the throne of King Renato d'Angiò, a cannonball burst into the church on October 17, 1439, heading in the direction of the sacred symbol. The figure of Christ supposedly bent his head and the cannonball damaged only his crown of thorns. With great devotion, the women of the historic city center still meet every Tuesday in front of the remains of St. Patricia in the attractive Baroque church of the convent of San Gregorio. A rich, noble and beautiful woman from distant parts, St. Patricia stripped herself of her worldly goods and dedicated her life to the city's poor.

For hundreds of years, workshops have opened directly onto the streets of the city center in which old craftsmen continue to demonstrate the skills they patiently learned as children by observing their fathers and listening to the secrets of their grandfathers, just as children still do today. They practice the art of the presepe or Christmas manger. Skilled hands give life to clay, modeling faces with expressive detail down to the last minuscule wrinkles, and fine fabrics are used for the clothes of the nobles, rags for those of the poor, and wood and cork for the houses and caves. In the Neapolitan mangers, the classic nativity scene is almost smothered by myriad contemporary references and personalities. It appears to be simply a means to open windows onto the world created around it in painstaking detail, including trattorias with crowded tables and plates of spaghetti, market stalls with fresh water sellers, fishmongers, and colorful fruit, hosts pouring wine, and water moving the mill wheels. A popular atmosphere, this is the bustling Naples of the eighteenth century recreated by master craftsmen summoned to court by kings who proudly displayed statuettes and cribs to foreign guests. The realm of the nativity scene craftsmen, invaded in the days leading up to Christmas by stalls full of statuettes, Via San Gregorio Armeno is one of the most important streets in the historic city center. It rises from Via San Biagio dei Librai, a section of the long Spaccanapoli (literally the Split of Naples) that traverses the city as straight as an arrow, and emerges on Via dei Tribunali, which in turn leads towards the imposing bulk of Castel Capuano where justice has been administered since the sixteenth century.

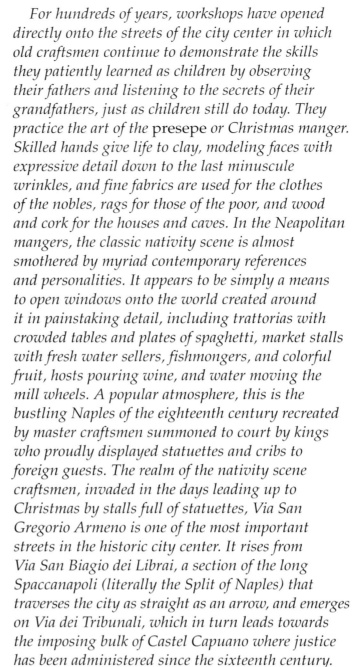

108 top The tradition of the presepe or Christmas manger became an art form in the eighteenth century when the sovereigns of Naples, sincere enthusiasts, summoned the master craftsmen of Via San Gregorio Armeno to court. The statuettes exhibited in the Royal Palace are part of the precious collection of the Fondazione Banco di Napoli.

108 center The daily life of the historic city center of Naples can be seen in numerous picturesque scenes: a barrow-boy sells flowers and a basket is lowered from a window in the classic way of doing the shopping without leaving the house.

108 bottom Some Neapolitan shops retain the atmosphere of bygone times, such as the fishmonger's under the portico on Via Tribunali that displays live fish in wooden tanks. The street onto which the shop faces follows the route of one of the two principal decumani of the ancient city.

108-109 One of the old carriages, almost all of which have now disappeared, passing in front of one of the statues of the kings located along the facade of the Royal Palace. These vehicles today take tourists on a romantic tour of the monuments in the center of Naples.

109 bottom A restorer concentrates on his craft in his workshop of sacred art. Many young craftsmen in the small workshops of the historic center of Naples have inherited the secrets of the trade handed down from father to son for centuries.

110 bottom left In order to find space to display his antiques and junk, the old shop of a second-hand dealer has expanded to the steps of a church in the labyrinthine lanes of the historic city center.

110 bottom right The bright red of Sorrento's cherry tomatoes and the glowing yellow of peppers, gourds, and corn cobs illuminate the wooden boxes and the entrance to a small greengrocer's.

111 top This photo perfectly captures the atmosphere of a typical local market, with the colorful stalls piled high with goods invading the narrow and crowded streets.

111 bottom Narrow lanes and white washing hung to dry in the sun, in the humblest quarters of Naples. These are the classic images that typify this complex metropolis.

110-111 An old knife-grinder works from door-to-door, traveling by bicycle. Old trades that have elsewhere disappeared survive in the precarious economy of the Neapolitan back streets.

112 The Neapolitans call the long street that, from Forcella to the hill of San Martino, cuts the historic city center in two, the "Spaccanapoli." Some of the most majestic churches, monumental piazzas, and elegant historic palaces face onto this principal urban artery.

113 top The Spire of San Gennaro was constructed to respect a vow by the Neapolitans who had invoked the saint's protection during the eruption of Vesuvius in 1631.

113 bottom The Hellenist statue of the Reclining Nile was found headless and for centuries the Neapolitans thought that it was the body of a woman. This conviction was shattered when the head, complete with a full beard, was discovered.

It is here, in fact, that the renowned Neapolitan legal system has its roots.

Beyond Castel Capuano stand the towers and gates of the fifteenth century Aragonese walls. Porta Capuana and Porta Nolana overlook the carnival colors and sounds of the lively fish and fruit markets. Among the streets there are traces of older constructions and Greek and Roman walls alongside beautiful piazzas, each with its church. The fourteenth century Santa Chiara is subtly elegant with its Gothic traits and a convent famed throughout the world for the beauty of the majolica decorating the Cloister of the Poor Clares.

114 top left The spire of Our Lady of the Immaculate Conception rises 98 feet high above Piazza del Gesù Nuovo in the old heart of the city. It was erected in 1748 in place of the equestrian statue of Philip V of Spain, demolished by popular demand.

114 bottom left The story goes that Francesco Petrarca lived in the convent of San Lorenzo Maggiore. A small door opens onto the cloister through which the undercroft with the remains of Roman workshops and older Greek structures can be reached.

114 top right The facade of the Baroque church of Trinità Maggiore, better known as the church of Jesù Nuovo, is in piperino, a kind of volcanic stone, dressed with a diamond-shaped nailhead motif.

114 bottom right The triumphant Renaissance arch of Porta Capuana is one of the entrances to the city opened in the Aragonese city walls.

115 The central door of the church of the Trinità Maggiore stands out, decorated with marble groups supported by columns of red granite, against the dark facade with its uniform nailhead motif.

116 In the Cloister of the Poor Clares of the Santa Chiara monastery, embellished with colored majolica, are two long avenues of vines and lemon trees.

117 left The typical colors of yellow, blue, and green of the magnificent majolica decoration of the Cloisters of Santa Chiara embellish the benches and the pillars that support the pergola of vines, with landscapes, scenes of country life, and imaginative figures.

117 top right The basilica of San Paolo Maggiore was built in the late sixteenth century on the site of the Roman Temple of the Dioscuri, of which a few columns still survive.

117 bottom right The terracotta statues of the Mourning of Christ group in the oratory of Santo Sepolcro are among the most precious treasures conserved in the fifteenth century church of Sant'Anna dei Lombardi, the favorite of the Aragonese royal family.

Simply cross the piazza to find radically different characteristics in the colored marble, great paintings, and Baroque opulence of the church of Gesù Nuovo. The treasures of Sant'Anna dei Lombardi, the favorite church of the Aragonese royal family, date from 1411. Columns that once belonged to the ancient temple of the Dioscuri today dominate the facade of the basilica of San Paolo Maggiore. Since the eighteenth century the little Sansevero Chapel has concealed the secrets of the alchemist prince, Raimondo di Sangro, inventor and necromancer, who was excommunicated for his experiments on cadavers. The veiled Christ however, is not, as popular tradition would have it, the body of a man covered with a mysterious substance as hard as marble and as translucent as opaque glass, but rather an incredible effect created by the sculptor Giuseppe Sammartino.

The churches are too many to list. Gothic, Renaissance, or Baroque, they are all beautiful and all contain a wealth of artistic treasures, tombs, and precious sculptures of kings, noblemen, and artists.

King Ladislao of Durazzo is mounted on horseback, proudly flourishing his unsheathed sword, an unusual activity in a church even for a statue. The great funerary monument was dedicated to him by his sister Joan II who succeeded him to the throne. Since then, the suggestive church of San Giovanni a Carbonara, dating back to 1343, has housed the remains of the last Anjou kings.

Religious buildings hold treasures such as the paintings of Mattia Preti kept in the church of San Pietro a Maiella, located in a street dedicated to

118-119 *The incredible effect obtained in the statue of the "Veiled Christ" should not be attributed to a mysterious experiment of the alchemist-prince, Raimondo di Sangro, as has been suggested in the past, but rather to the artistic talent of the sculptor Giuseppe Sammartino.*

119 top The ancient noble chapel of Sansevero is associated in popular tradition with the story and the mysteries of the alchemist-prince, Raimondo di Sangro. Thanks to him, in the eighteenth century the construction became one of the most important monuments in the Naples of the time.

119 bottom Like the better known "Veiled Christ," the statue of Modesty by the artist Antonio Corradini, conserved in the Sansevero Chapel, appears to be covered in a petrified veil, an effect that has always excited the popular imagination.

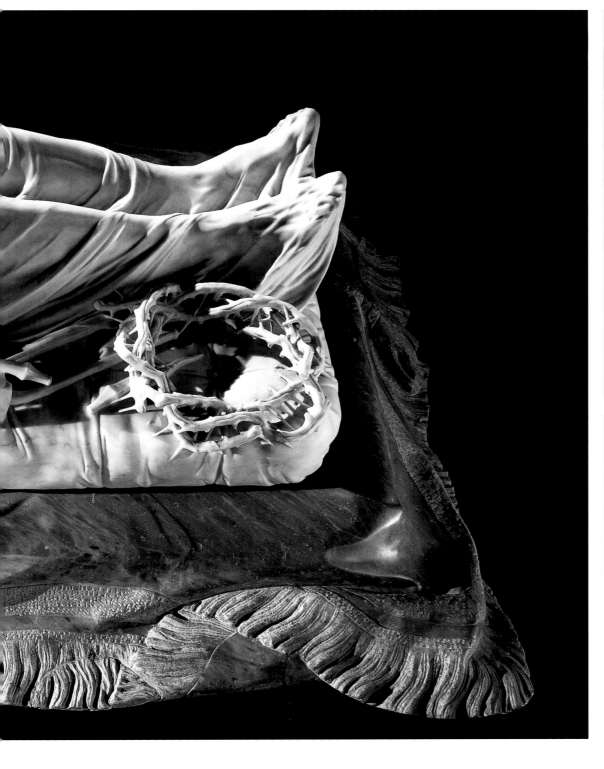

120 left In the magnificent church of San Giovanni a Carbonara, King Ladislau is seen on horseback, brandishing a sword, in the funerary monument dedicated to him by his sister, Joan II, who succeeded him to the throne in 1414.

120 top right The Caracciolo del Sole Chapel in the fourteenth century church of San Giovanni a Carbonara, is completely decorated with fifteenth century frescoes and features a floor of magnificent majolica tiles.

music since the nineteenth century when the conservatory was installed in a former convent. The suffering of the people in the labyrinth streets of the seventeenth century can be seen in the masterpiece by Michelangelo da Caravaggio on the altar of the church of Pio Monte della Misericordia. Always an institution ready to welcome the needy, the ample portico, an architectural feature unusual in the city center, provided a roof for the homeless. The histories of ancient institutions, architectural masterpieces rich in works of art, are closely bound to the drama of a population that has always known hunger and poverty.

Among them is the Santissima Casa dell'Annunziata, with a bell, a small door just large enough for the body of a new-born baby and a wheel. By turning the wheel unmarried mothers and desperate parents retained their anonymity while, with a last caress, their offspring passed beyond the wall into trusted hands. Objects were pawned to pay debts and prayers were offered in

120 bottom right The tomb of Ser Gianni Caracciolo, supported by three warriors, is found behind the altar of the church of San Giovanni a Carbonara. The ambitious nobleman, the lover of Joan II, was stabbed to death in the corridors of Castel Capuano.

121 In the so-called "Seven Works of Mercy" painted by Caravaggio, all the drama of popular life in seventeenth century Naples appears. This painting is the most suggestive of the works in the chapel of the ancient charitable institution of Pio Monte della Misericordia.

122 *Charity and Security stand out among the paintings on the frescoed ceiling of the Chapel of Pio Monte di Pietà. The institute issued loans on reasonable terms to counter the plague of usury.*

123 top *The Chapel of Monte di Pietà, built in the courtyard of an austere palace dating from the early seventeenth century, boasts fine frescoes, gilded stucco work and large paintings.*

123 bottom *The shelves in walnut and briar of the eighteenth century pharmacy of the Ospedale degli Incurabili, contain valuable ceramic jars decorated with biblical and allegorical scenes.*

the beautiful chapel of the Monte di Pietà invoking better times.

The Compagnia dei Bianchi della Giustizia assisted those condemned to death in the chapel of the sixteenth century hospital for the terminally ill. Here, fabulous ceramic jars and beautifully decorated shelves make the Pharmacy an eighteenth century masterpiece.

Today, on special occasions, there is a one-way system for pedestrians to regulate the flow of visitors to the streets of the "open-air museum." Recently rediscovered, the historic center has been revived and the café tables have returned to the most attractive piazzas.

Naples invites one to stroll through history, along streets that conceal a secret: the undersoil of the city is a cultural treasure chest containing traces of its distant past. It hides buried cities, caves and tunnels, and crypts and catacombs. The Greeks dug the first shafts four centuries before Christ, sinking them up to 230 feet deep to reach the layer of tuff, a rock so friable as to be workable with chisels. They extracted the large squared blocks which were used to build the first city walls. The process continued for centuries and centuries as each building had its own shaft. For the city to grow, stone had to be extracted from under its very foundations. From the remotest of times up to the present day, the abandoned quarries became great cisterns linked by narrow tunnels that carried the city's water supply. The oldest subterranean aqueduct dates from the third century B.C. and runs for five miles from Vesuvius to each of the houses of the original Greek colony. There are 800 known cavities and 6,000 shafts. During the Second World War and the bombing raids on Naples, the population sought refuge in these labyrinth tunnels. Day after day, they

waited and prayed. Today they are visited by tourists who descend 250 steps into the great halls of yellow stone and walk by candlelight along the high, narrow passages.

The church of San Lorenzo Maggiore is truly beautiful in solemn Franciscan style. It was here that in 1334 Boccaccio met Fiametta and a few years later Francesco Petrarca came to seek refuge and pray after being terrified by a tidal wave. From the choir it is possible to follow a steep, narrow staircase to a few feet below street level to discover more streets and small workshops. Like a miniature Pompeii, the Macellum and the Aerarium were part of the Roman city dating from the year 100 and were buried in the fifth century under mud after a flood. The opus reticulatum typical of the Roman walls rests on the stones of the Greek city of Neapolis, with its grand theater. This is the great secret of underground Naples, not simply galleries and caves, but also entire cities constructed one on top of another, churches superimposed over earlier churches. The city, grew in layers, the new covering rather than erasing the old. Thus, the wood-fired oven of the Roman city of two thousand years ago corresponds precisely, eight feet lower down, with the almost identical oven of the pizzeria that for a century has occupied a street-corner position. After a further short stroll through the lanes, there are fresh flowers and lighted candles next to a bronze skull. In the crypt below the Church of the Purgatorio ad Arco survives an ancient cult officially banned by the church.

A flower and a prayer is offered for the anime pezzentelle, or homeless souls, people who died with neither tomb nor name.

Those skulls and those bones found in the common graves of catacombs and crypts perform minor miracles to satisfy the simple wishes of the poorest people. The "Head of Lucia," a woman of noble birth who died in the seventeenth century after falling in love with a commoner, wears a wedding veil. Girls looking for a husband or desiring a son offer their prayers to her whereas mothers worried about the health a little one caress the skull of a child. The same cult can be found in the crypt of the church of San Pietro ad Aram and in the ancient Sanità quarter where, on the slopes of the Capodimonte hill, the Greeks excavated underground tombs in which to bury their dead and the early Christians dug catacombs and chapels. In the seventeenth century those great caves became the cemeteries of the poor and the plague-stricken. The ossuary of the Fontanelle contains the remains of eight million dead where mountains of bones, were piously gathered into ordered piles during the nineteenth century. Since then those poor souls have been adopted by the people of Naples, and certain skulls chosen and set on small altars bear witness to stories of everyday troubles, dream and requests for help, often involving the winning lottery numbers.

124-125 The suggestive Catacombs of San Gennaro were used for burials from the second century through the ducal age. The subsoil of Naples conserves the wonders of a subterranean city excavated in the tuff since time immemorial.

125 top The undercrofts of old churches contain ancient treasures, such as the Cristallini Hypogeum, dating from the fourth century B.C. which is reached via a church in the Sanità quarter.

125 bottom Great caves open up in the subsoil of Naples, linked to the surface via shafts to the courtyards of the old palaces. During distant eras, and for centuries, the blocks of tuff used for building were not brought in to the city but quarried on the spot.

Ancient history, popular beliefs and life are entwined in a city that today, ready for the challenge of the new frontiers, opens its doors to Europe, puts itself forwards as a bridge between diverse cultures in the role of a Mediterranean capital, and establishes and reinforces close ties with the rest of the world. The meeting of the G7 heads of state in 1994 marked a turning point and sparked tangible improvement in the city's image and quality of life over the last few years. A city with distant roots that has been martyred by plagues, poverty, and crime, it proudly has proved capable of change while remaining true to itself. The Naples of the new millennium is no longer the city of just ten years ago and is completing the latest in a series of minor revolutions. The churches whose doors had been walled up because bricks and mortar were the precious furnishings and rare masterpieces' only defence against thieves have been reopened. Buses run almost on time, pay parking lots have appeared, vigilant traffic wardens patrol and issue fines, tour buses come and go, and uniformed police officers are on the beat. None of these things should be taken for granted but should rather be seen as great conquests for this instinctively rebellious city.

Today, the vast Piazza Plebiscito, elegant and embraced by the colonnade of the church of San Francesco di Paola facing the noble facade of the Royal Palace redesigned by Vanvitelli, is the symbol of the new Naples, the setting for concerts broadcast across Europe and the first Neapolitan New Year's Eve to be celebrated in the street, all together under the raining fireworks, rather than at home with the family. Just a few years ago it was nothing more than an immense, chaotic and depressing expanse of parked cars. In the vicinity of the piazza are other treasures such as Piazza Trento and Trieste, previously named Piazza San Ferdinando, where a nameless church sits in the center and the historic Caffè Gambrinus, long a meeting place for artists, poets and writers boasts splendid nineteenth century stucco work, mirrors, and frescoes.

126 top The impressive neo-classical church of San Francesco di Paola was erected as a votive offering by Ferdinand I when he retook his kingdom from the French.

126 bottom Narrow and tall, the houses in Via Chiaia mark the confine between the elegant shopping streets and the intricate labyrinth of lanes in the Spanish Quarters.

126-127 *The Piazza del Plebiscito, today a symbol of a city that has rediscovered its treasures, is immense. The church of San Francesco di Paola, seen in this photo, and the Royal Palace both face onto the square.*

127 bottom Since the nineteenth century, the historic Caffè Gambrinus in Piazza Trieste e Trento, beloved of Gabriele D'Annunzio, has been a meeting place for intellectuals and artists.

128 top left The facade of the Royal Palace and the Teatro San Carlo act as the backdrop to the dome and the entrance to the Galleria Umberto I that, beyond Piazza Trieste e Trento, dominates the view from Piazza del Plebiscito.

128 bottom left Pulcinella accompanies with the romantic music of a mandolin a newly-wed couple who have chosen the sophisticated interior of the Galleria for their wedding photographs.

128 center Delicate marble inlays compose the variously colored decoration of the floor of the Galleria, setting off the gilded stucco work of the interior facades.

128 right The Galleria, which once housed the Café Chantant of the Salone Margherita, is still today the traditional meeting point for out-of-work artists in search of engagements.

129 Great copper angels support the glass and iron dome of the Galleria Umberto I, a late nineteenth century masterpiece designed by the engineer Paolo Boubée. The structure has a cruciform plan and is a little over 184 feet high.

The imposing bulk of the Palazzo Reale, the Royal Palace, extends with terraces and gardens, to overlook the sea. Designed in the seventeenth century by Domenico Fontana, it features art and opulence in the royal apartments, jewels such as the Little Theater and the Court Chapel, one wing which now houses the National Library. Next door, the Neapolitan temple of opera, the Teatro San Carlo, was inaugurated on November 4, 1737, on Charles of Bourbon's saint's day and dedicated to the saint. Facing the opera house, the Galleria Umberto I, a nineteenth century salon of French inspiration with beautifully decorated facades, towers over elegant palaces. Music seems to rise magically from the gratings among the fine mosaics of the floor up towards the glass and iron dome supported by great angels. In a large subterranean hall, the Cinématographe Lumière *made its Neapolitan debut in 1896, and the Salone Margherita, a Neapolitan-style singing* cafè, *provided the sound track to the* belle époque.

130 top Large tapestries, woven locally and in France, paintings, furniture, and bronzes in the imperial style embellish the Hall of the Ambassadors in the Royal Palace.

130 bottom The majestic main staircase, with its double flights of steps set amid sculptures and glittering colored marble, provides guests with an ideal introduction to the opulence of the apartments in Naples' Royal Palace.

130-131 This aerial photo shows the imposing lateral facade of the Royal Palace, overlooking the Molosiglio Gardens, a step away from the sea.

131 bottom left The seventeenth century chapel dedicated to Our Lady of the Assumption, located at the heart of the historic apartments of the Royal Palace, is perhaps the most suggestive of the majestic building's architectural jewels.

131 bottom right Bas-reliefs with the symbols and images of the twelve provinces of the Kingdom of Naples decorate the ceiling of the Throne Room in the Royal Palace, the walls of which are hung with portraits of the sovereigns. The throne, carrying the eagle symbol of the Savoy family, stands beneath the eighteenth century canopy.

132-133 The interior of the Teatro San Carlo as seen from the stage reveals all its stately elegance. The Royal Box is located in the center while the 184 other boxes are set on six levels. Apollo presents the greatest Greek, Latin, and Italian Poets to Minerva in the painting by Giuseppe Cammarano decorating the ceiling.

A short distance away are the five powerful turrets
of Castel Nuovo, which the Neapolitans prefer to call
Maschio Angioino, a fourteenth century castle by the
sea. Here Ferdinand II staged a fake marriage, inviting
all the principle barons of the kingdom: Guitly of
plotting against him, the barons left the castle in
chains, their scheme exposed. On the portal, amid the
walls of dark stone, the white Arch of Triumph stands
out marking the advent of the Aragon dynasty. A
tribute to Alfonso I, this is one of the most beautiful
works of the Neapolitan renaissance. The huge and
terrible crocodile that lived in a moat below the jail,
the guilty party in the mysterious disappearance of
numerous prisoners, above all those considered to be
"inconvenient," was stuffed and hung on the arch until
halfway through the nineteenth century. The port opens
at the base of the walls and provides a haven for some
of the world's greatest cruise liners. Tourists quickly
disembark for a fleeting glance at the monuments and
the shop windows of Via Roma and Via Chiaia, the
nearby shopping streets. Behind the port, a hill
overlooks this corner of Naples, with a garden that
climbs amid flowering wisteria and pergolas with
ancient vines up towards the porticoes of the white
Certosa of San Martino (although housing the precious
collection of the Museum of the Kingdom of Naples, the
Neapolitans are particularly fond of it for its attractive
eighteenth century Christmas manger). Elegant and

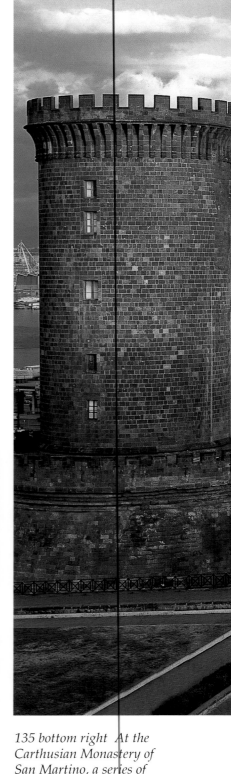

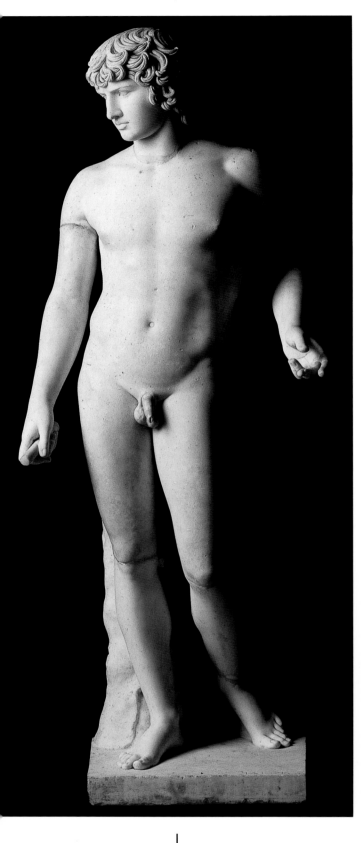

unimposing, its back is protected by the powerful wall of the invincible fortress of Castel Sant'Elmo which dominates the entire city. Its cannons once stood ready to subdue any revolt but today it hosts shows and major art exhibitions.

The focal point of the history of Neapolitan art is instead the Capodimonte Museum, yet another palace immersed in the greenery of a large park that Charles of Bourbon built during the eighteenth century. Thanks to the important exhibits of recent years which have featured masterpieces of leading Neapolitan artists through the centuries, and have been rewarded with a record-breaking stream of visitors, an extremely significant contribution has been made to Naples' cultural rebirth.

The oldest history is contained in the prestigious Palazzo degli Studi which although originally built in 1585 as stables, became the university in the seventeenth century and a museum when in 1777 Ferdinand IV was looking for a worthy home for the masterpieces of the Farnese collection and the relics discovered at Herculaneum and Pompeii. Over time, important private collections have been added, along with artifacts from some of the most important archaeological digs of southern Italy. Today, the National Archaeological Museum, which stands imposing and sober in front of the gilded stucco work of the Galleria Principe di Napoli, is in terms of the wealth of its exhibits, the most important museum of ancient art in the South.

138 left and 139 The beauty of Antinoo lies in the rare purity of line in the details of the face of this marble sculpture. The work, which represents the young favorite of the emperor Hadrian, a cult object after his premature death, is one of the relics in the Farnese collection conserved in the Archaeological Museum of Naples.

138 right The drama of the battle is described with great emotive force in the celebrated mosaic depicting The Battle of Issus which, almost 20 feet wide, decorated the floor of the House of the Faun in Pompeii.

140 In the exceptional collection of marble sculpture in the National Archaeological Museum of Naples, there are many Roman copies of works, in many cases now lost, from the classical and Hellenist periods. The original of the Farnese Hercules, found at Rome in the Caracalla Baths, was a bronze by Lysippus from the fourth century B.C.

141 The group of the Tyrannicides, Harmodius and Aristogiton, among the museum's most famous works, is a copy of the bronzes of Kritios and Nesiotes from 477 B.C.

*142 top The University of
Naples was founded by
Frederick II around 1220.
The Minerva Steps links
the central building with the
Via Mezzocannone complex.*

*142 bottom The Pompeiano
Salon is one of the refined
historical rooms at
Capodimonte. The great
palace, which immediately
became a museum, houses
precious collections.*

*142-143 A thousand crystal
droplets of two enormous
chandeliers glitter in the
spacious ball room of the
royal residence at
Capodimonte.*

*143 bottom The greenery
of the large park frames the
severe red facade with grey
piperino pillars of the
Capodimonte palace, built
at the behest of Charles of
Bourbon in 1738.*

Of particular note are the groups of marble sculptures, mainly Roman copies of classical and Hellenist originals, such as the Tyrannicides, Harmodius and Aristogiton, Polycletus' Doryphorus, found at Pompeii, the Farnese Hercules and the imposing group of the Bull from the Baths of Caracalla. The Tablets of Heraclea (late fourth century B.C.) with laws, distance tables, boundary stones, and calendars testifies to the oldest administration of this land and the phases of its Romanisation. And there is also an important example of ancient Egyptian history with relics that came from the eighteenth century collections of the Borgia and Picchianti families.

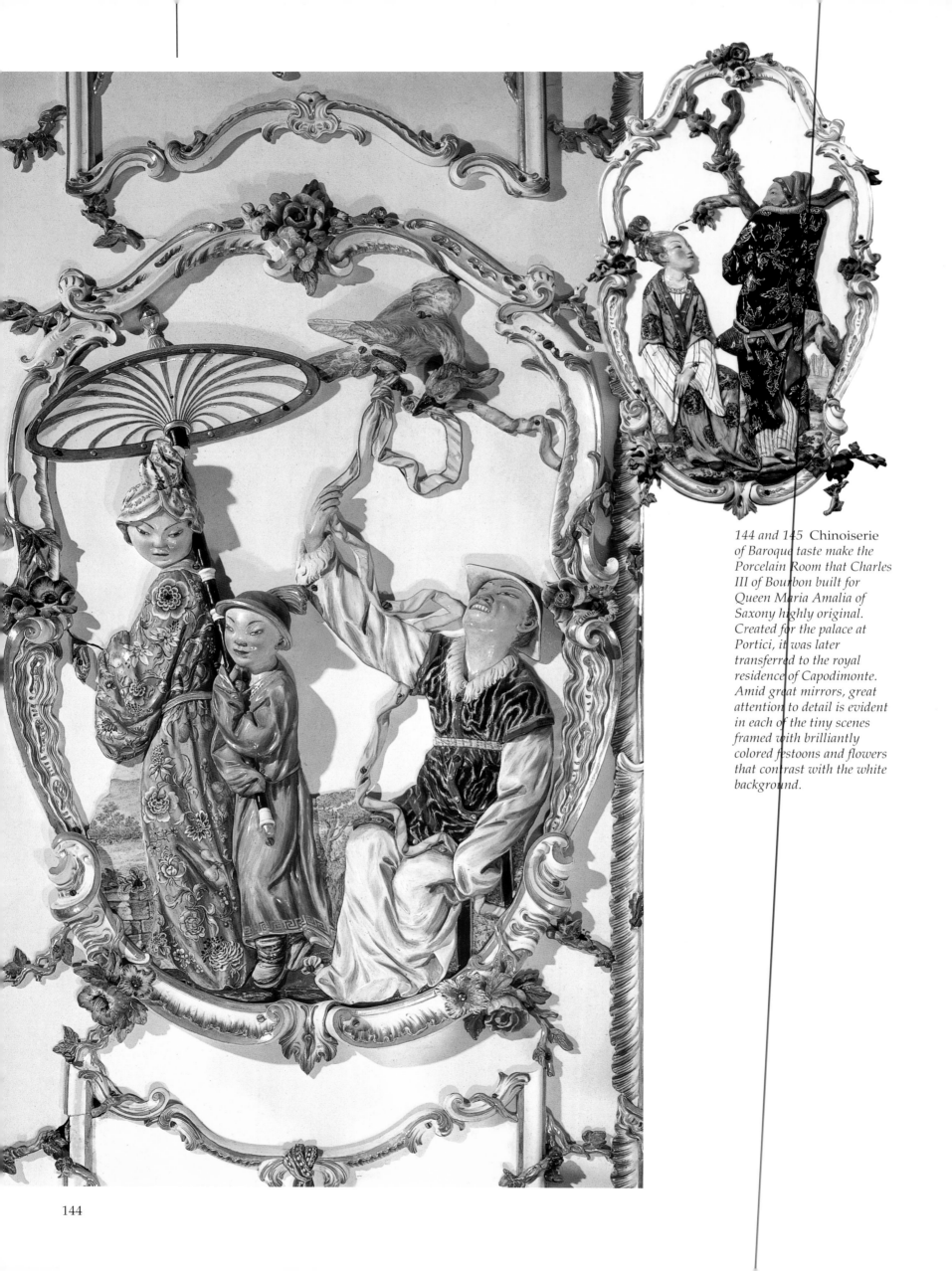

144 and 145 Chinoiserie of Baroque taste make the Porcelain Room that Charles III of Bourbon built for Queen Maria Amalia of Saxony highly original. Created for the palace at Portici, it was later transferred to the royal residence of Capodimonte. Amid great mirrors, great attention to detail is evident in each of the tiny scenes framed with brilliantly colored festoons and flowers that contrast with the white background.

Naples is Italy's third largest city after Milan and Rome. It has significant plans: the obsolete chimneys of the steel-making area of Bagnoli, on the shore looking out towards Cape Miseno, has today been transformed from a depressing symbol of lost jobs in a city that is a capital of unemployment to a symbol of rebirth thanks to a radical program to promote tourism which has restored what is one of the most attractive stretches of coastline.

Naples' history is complex. The Greek colonists founded Palaepolis, the ancient city, seven centuries before Christ, and Neapolis, the new city, three centuries later. Another hundred years later they surrendered to the Romans. The Lombards arrived in the 500s, followed by the Normans. And then there were the Swabians: Frederick II founded the university in 1224. The Angevin kings ruled from

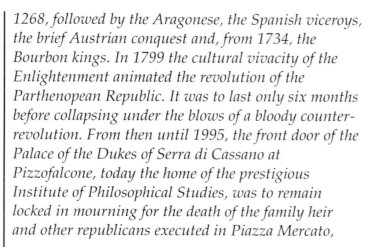

1268, followed by the Aragonese, the Spanish viceroys, the brief Austrian conquest and, from 1734, the Bourbon kings. In 1799 the cultural vivacity of the Enlightenment animated the revolution of the Parthenopean Republic. It was to last only six months before collapsing under the blows of a bloody counter-revolution. From then until 1995, the front door of the Palace of the Dukes of Serra di Cassano at Pizzofalcone, today the home of the prestigious Institute of Philosophical Studies, was to remain locked in mourning for the death of the family heir and other republicans executed in Piazza Mercato,

a symbol of the silent dissent of a class of aristocrats and men of culture.

It is a history of continual outside domination. A history of one of the few cities in Europe, like Rome or Paris, to have endured for three thousand years without fail, steadfastly true to the heart of its original stones. The Greeks laid those stones on Mount Echia, a small hill not far from the shoreline where a row of the city's most elegant hotels now looks towards the Castel dell'Ovo, with Borgo Marinari and the small port of Santa Lucia at the foot of the fortifications that rise from the sea, with the tables of its bars, simple

146 top The semicircle to be seen halfway up Via Nazario Sauro includes the monument dedicated to King Umberto I and the Immacolatella fountain, the latter in part the work of Bernini.

146 bottom Castel dell'Ovo dominates the houses of the Borgo Marinari quarter. On the horizon the island of Capri can be seen, in an enchanting view from the shore.

146-147 The powerful stone bastions of Castel dell'Ovo rise above the sea and overlook the small port of Santa Lucia on the small island of Megaride.

147 bottom The most luxurious cruise ships dock in the port of Naples. The rebirth of tourism is a recent conquest for a city that has invested heavily in the revitalization of long neglected resources.

148-149 The sea at Mergellina reflects the lively colors of the typical wooden fishing boats in a village-like atmosphere. This is, in fact, one of the corners of Naples that belie being in a major city.

148 bottom Behind the wharf of Riva Fiorita, along the coast of Posillipo, nature embraces Villa Rosebery, the favorite official residence of recent presidents of Italian Republic.

trattorias, and celebrated restaurants. The castle and fort were built on the tiny island of Megaride where legend has it that the siren Parthenope allowed herself to die, and the sea breeze carried far and wide the aromas of the legendary table of the general Lucius Licinius Lucullus. A Norman fortress, Castel dell'Ovo was progressively enlarged as it passed from noble to noble. It was once a prison in which Conrad of Swabia and the sons of Manfred were held. It was also the noble residence of kings: Alfonso of Aragon, enchanted by those lines, those powerful external fortifications, those sweet medieval views and the terraces on the sea within the walls, chose it as the place in which he would await his death. In its foundations, it was said during the Middle Ages, Virgil placed an egg. When the egg breaks the walls purportedly will crumble and the entire city will be plagued by misfortune.

From here the gentle curve of the sea grazes the greenery of the Royal Walk at Chiaia, today the Villa Comunale. Beyond the port of Mergellina the coast slowly begins to climb, up through the green and silent hills of Posillipo to the cape where the Virgiliano park watches the sun tinge the sky red before disappearing behind Cape Miseno. High on the small island of Gaiola, and on the Trentaremi Bay, those caves with lines too natural to have been drawn by Mother Nature, are actually tunnels excavated by the Romans. The 2625 foot-long Grotto di Seiano once led, a hundred years before Christ, to the stunning Villa Pausilypon of Vedius Pollione in a treasure chest of tuff by the sea.

A thousand times the landscapists of the celebrated School of Posillipo have depicted the apparently ruined noble edifice, with its three facades rising suggestively directly from the sea. Palazzo donn'Anna was the love nest of the Spanish viceroy, Don Ramiro Guzman, Duke of Medina della Torres, and the beautiful noblewoman, Anna Carafa. The story did not have a happy ending, and he soon returned to Spain, while she died, not yet thirty years old, leaving the palazzo unfinished. It is said that her ghost still roams its halls. It is also said that it subsequently became the haven for the licentious encounters of Queen Giovanna. In the rooms overlooking the sea wander the spirits of the fishermen seduced by the queen before being killed.

Beautiful villas and ancient villages can be discovered anywhere in this area. The neo-classical Villa Rosebery, the residence of the President of the Republic, is set in a park of holly trees and magnolias. A few houses cluster around the church of Santa Maria del Faro, and tiny fishing boats are moored among the rocks. If it was not for the lights of the restaurants on a hundred terraces overlooking the sea, the atmosphere would be even more akin to that of the celebrated fenestella in the verses of Salvatore di Giacomo: a small window, geranium flowers, and a romantic view as the moons rises.

149 top The traffic and offices of the city center are close by, but life passes at a different rhythm in the small port of Mergellina where, day after day, the fishermen patiently repair their nets.

149 bottom The wooden boats at Mergellina create a colorful platform on the sea. The nets, laid out on the pier, are ready for fishing, while Vesuvius appears to watch over the labors of the Bay of Naples fishermen.

Naples remains an unstoppable city offers excitement at every corner. Poetry and songs in dialect recall an age-old tradition, which inspired unforgettable melodies written by enthusiastic locals as well as artists of the caliber of Vincenzo Bellini and Gaetano Donizetti. O sole mio is still heard throughout the world. How could the cross-sections of real life presented in the immortal theater of the De Filippo brothers and Raffaele Viviani ever be forgotten? Revolutionary cinema in the form of the explosive comedy of the remarkable Totò, the films of Vittorio De Sica, the screen icon Sophia Loren and the up-and-coming directors and actors of the present day continue to delight spectators. Painting, architecture, literature, schools, art and culture have without fail characterized Naples along with more simple forms of culture such as story of Pulcinella's mask or pizza Margherita. The Neapolitan sweets, venerable and imaginative recipes including sfogliatelle, babà, struffoli, mustaccioli, susamielli, rococò, the classic pastiera and the zeppole of San Giuseppe, and the Santa Rosa, are part of a tradition of good cooking that is renewed on a daily basis. The aroma of the ragù (a meat sauce) rises like a flag every Sunday morning. Spaghetti, paccheri, ziti pasta is sacred and reigns supreme over mere sandwiches. Even during a lunch break one eats as if Mamma had cooked.

Recounting Naples, and doing it well, is impossible. There are too many faces and too many contradictions. It is only possible to sketch impressions and perhaps capture one aspect or another, whereas it is impossible to describe the city with the presumption of having captured its essence. This is a city to be experienced while, breathing its air and sampling its atmosphere. Everyone will see it in a different way, no one will be wrong. Each time Naples may look at the visitor with different eyes, but it will always be sincere.

150 top The architectural trail of Neapolitan art nouveau winds between elegant palaces and well-tended gardens, from Via Tasso along Corso Vittorio Emanuele, slowly descending the hillside.

150 bottom In the little fishing village built on the rocks at Marechiaro, the finestrella, or little window, known throughout the world thanks to the poetry of Salvatore di Giacomo, not only provides a romantic sea view but is a symbol of the rich tradition of Neapolitan song.

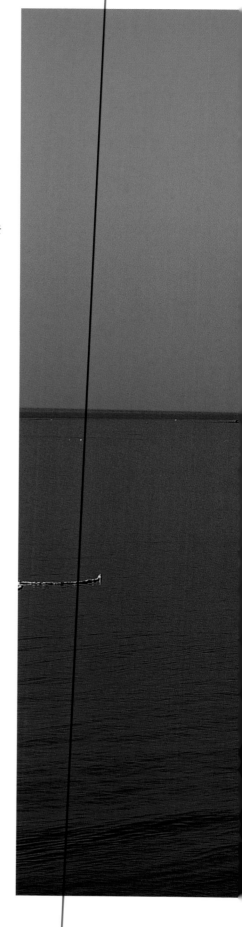

150-151 Palazzo donn'Anna is reflected in the sea of Posillipo. The air of mystery about its unfinished facades has inspired stories of love, murder, and ghosts, handed down from generation to generation.

151 bottom The terraces of the Virgiliano Park overlook the sea surrounding the small island of Nisida and, further away beyond the bay of Pozzuoli, look out towards Cape Miseno, Procida, and Ischia.

CASERTA, BENEVENTO, AVELLINO AND SALERNO:
TIMID BEAUTIES

*152 top The stone towers
and walls of medieval
Caserta rise lonely in the
woods at the top of a hill
overlooking the new town.*

Back in the last years of the eighteenth century
there was nothing but a tiny village around an
ancient tower on a plain chosen to be the site of the
construction of a great royal palace at Caserta,
intended to be the pride of the Bourbon kings. Built
at the behest of Charles III, distant nephew of the
Sun King of France, the palace was intended to be
so beautiful as to rival Versailles. All around were
the first few houses of a new city that was to grow
swiftly. Today it is the provincial capital.

The Caserta of more distant times is a short
distance away, a small medieval village built by
the Lombards in the seventh century, perched
on a hill and clustering around the attractive
cathedral dating from 1100, nowadays little changed
and known as Caserta Vecchia.

The flood plain of the River Volturno, a cradle
of antiquity, is but a step away. Here, where
the Oscans and the Samnites left traces of
civilizations dating back over three thousand years,
the Etruscans produced precious carpets, vases
in bronze, and black ceramic to trade with the
first Greek colonies on the coast of Campania,
such as Capua which became the largest and
wealthiest city of the region in the Roman empire.

Small and peaceful, despite its modern appearance
and rapid expansion, Caserta still seems to be an
unfocused backdrop to the Bourbon palace. The long
Corso Trieste is the lively fulcrum of daily life, along
with the cafes in Piazza Vanvitelli and the nineteenth
century Piazza del Duomo, but the great palace
imposes itself on every view and welcomes those
arriving in the city as it dominates the endless
avenue giving access to the town, mile after mile,
standing out like a guiding beacon. The surrounding
city only appears after getting up close to it.

It is an extraordinary building. Charles III of
Bourbon erred on the side of excess when he chose to
challenge the French court. He commissioned a well
known architect, Luigi Vanvitelli, and work was to be
in progress for the next 22 years. Four courtyards,
five floors, 1,200 rooms were constructed at vast
expense: six million ducats was no small sum. The

*152 bottom A ring of hills
embraces the immense plain
extending around the city of
Caserta. A number of small
villages punctuate the empty
spaces untouched by cement.*

*152-153 The harmony of colors
and finely rendered decorations
makes the twelfth-century
cathedral in Caserta a
masterpiece. The Romanesque
building has elements of
Pugliese and Arab-Sicilian
architecture, and was inspired
by the nearby Duomo of Sessa
Aurunca. The bell-tower rises
above a 105-foot arch that
straddles one of the ancient
stone streets of the city.*

*153 bottom The red wine of the
countryside between Caserta
and Benevento is much sought
after. In the Maddaloni Valley,
well-known for its local
annuche apples, esteemed
vineyards lie among the trees.*

entire fief of Caserta had been acquired for less than five hundred thousand. The available labor force was not sufficient and the king even put the inmates of the jail to work. Furthermore, he summoned to court a small army of major and minor artists. The great staircase is an architectural masterpiece and King Charles is seen here sculpted in marble ready to welcome his guests on the back of the symbolic lion of power. Among the other statues are those of Merit and Truth. The royal apartments are a triumph of stucco work, marble, bas-reliefs, frescoed vaults, tapestries, and precious furnishings. The Palantine Chapel is clearly inspired by the style of "rival" Versailles, but there is a typically Neapolitan atmosphere in the Court Theater where the music of the Neapolitan school of Cimarosa and Paisello was perfomed.

154 top left *Framed by vegetation, the suggestive avenue traversing the park of the Royal Palace of Caserta leads the gaze to the imposing Vanvitellian facade.*

154 bottom left *The Peschiera Grande, or Great Fish Pond, lies between ordered avenues and traces a patchwork of green in the vast royal park.*

154-155 *This aerial photo reveals the opulence and elegance that formed the basis of Vanvitelli's design for the Royal Palace of Caserta, in accordance with the wishes of Charles III of Bourbon. The sovereign, engaging in a form of rivalry with the Sun King in France, wanted a summer residence that would overshadow even Versailles.*

King Charles was not satisfied with all this architectural beauty. The true scenestealer is the huge garden containing fish ponds, waterfalls, and running water that leaps from pool to pool, laps the feet of marble statues, and descends through groves of trees. There is Dolphin Cascade, the Aeolus Fountain with the 29 statues of the winds, the Ceres Spring, the twelve cascades of the fountain of Venus and Adonis. A nearly two-mile long prospect of greenery and water leads the gaze to the distant great waterfall that from the top of a hill plunges to the rocks and statues of the pool where Diana,

surrounded by nymphs, defeats Actaeon who, transformed into a stag, is eaten by his own dogs. The water arrives from distant Mount Taburno, along a 25-mile long aqueduct that overcomes valleys and mountains and tunnels through five mountains, a work as bold as the 1736-feet long Valle Bridges between Mount Longano and Mount Calvi at Maddaloni, all to bring water to the garden of the king.

It is said that Ferdinand IV (Charles had acceded to the throne of Spain) waited impatiently for four hours for the water to complete the full distance on

155 top right The marvelous play of water in a series of fountains, fish ponds, and marble sculptural groups set on banks and rocks lends a unique look to the immense avenue that leads from the Royal Palace to the Great Fountain.

155 bottom right Diana, in a chorus of nymphs, is immortalized in the act of crushing Actaeon. Various

scenes inspired by the myth are represented in the fountain into which the Great Cascade falls from a height of 256 feet. The water is brought a great distance by means of the Carolino Aqueduct.

156-157 In terms of a romantic setting, in addition to a cultural one, the Reggia is without doubt the most thrilling and splendid sight in all of Campania.

158 and 159 left Paintings, stucco-work, marble, frescoes, bas-reliefs, and fine furniture; the opulence reaches exceptional levels in the monumental royal apartments in the palace at Caserta, considered to be an architectural masterpiece. The rooms are of various sizes and functions, including the ten of the Apartment of the King, the large rooms of the Old Apartment, and the three of the New Apartment. Large halls, the Palantine Chapel, and the court theater complete the Royal Palace.

159 top right Twelve bas-reliefs illustrate episodes from the Iliad in the Mars Salon. This room, in the imperial style, is one of the three composing the New Apartment, so-called because it was one of the last to be completed in long realization of the Royal Palace of Caserta.

159 bottom right The 116 steps of the grand staircase lead, in an introduction to the marvels to come, to the Apartment of the King. A space created in the ceiling housed musicians who, while remaining concealed, poured out a stream of notes upon His Majesty's entrance.

the day of his inauguration, May 7, 1762.

All around the great park are woods and ponds, as well as a 62-acre botanical garden designed by a Briton, Andrea Grafer, for Maria Carolina of Austria. Among rare plants around the swan lake, the first camellia blossomed in Europe. On a single day each year, Easter Monday, the park was opened to the subjects who joyously poured in for the traditional Easter banquet offered by the king. The court transferred here from Naples in Autumn and Spring. Those periods saw continuous receptions, hunting parties, music performances, and shows. Artists and the literati were at home here, including fond guests such as Wolfgang Goethe.

Though among the most conservative, the Bourbon dynasty attempted a form of socialist experiment. Ferdinand IV designed his "Ferdinandopolis" a few miles from the palace, where the Royal Belvedere Shooting Lodge had been constructed for the hunting parties, in the village that took its name from the old Lombard church dedicated to San Leucio. By royal warrant it became a colony for masters of the art of working with the most precious silk. It was an independent community based on extraordinarily innovative rules: parity among all members of the colony, even between men and women, including questions of inheritance, obligatory schooling, the abolition of dowries, and an absolute ban on parents interfering with the sentimental affairs and marriage plans of their offspring.

160 top The landscape changes to the north of Caserta where the great plain of Campania gives way to the hills that rise steeply towards the Matese mountain range.

160 bottom Thanks to the Bridges of the Valley at Maddaloni, the long aqueduct bringing water to the gardens of the Royal Palace at Caserta crosses the 1736 feet of a gorge between the mountains. This great feat of civil engineering was the result of one of the many kingly caprices recorded by history.

A strong agricultural tradition characterized the province and especially the flood plain of the River Volturno ever since the first Italic settlements of three thousand years ago. Since the medieval era it has been known as the "Terra di Lavoro," or "Land of Work," fertile and hence often fought over. It was the theater for many epic battles. Once Etruscan, the Romans colonized it and Capua became a wealthy but rebellious colony along the strategic Via Appia. History recalls the period of rest spent by Hannibal and the revolt of the gladiator Spartacus at the head of an army of slaves.

There followed the barbarian invasions, the strong kingdom of the Lombards, and the Norman settlements. A not inconsiderable contribution, as legend has it, was made to the cuisine of Campania by the monks of Capua who in 1100, created for the first time a certain form of stringy cheese, during the making of which they had to plunge their hands into boiling water. This was buffalo-milk mozzarella, the pride and joy of the region. In recent history the region was also the most important link in the unification of Italy. Garibaldi met Vittorio Emanuele II at Teano in order to hand over the south of Italy.

The ancient colony of Capua, abandoned after the Saracen incursion of 841, is today Santa Maria Capua Vetere. The new Capua was founded on the ruins of the small Roman river port of Casilinum.

Of the opulence of times long past remains the great amphitheater. With its three arched tiers of travertine decorated with statues and a fourth closed tier that reach a total height of 151 feet, only the Coliseum in Rome is bigger. Elegant with the broad colonnade built at the behest of Hadrian, it

160-161 Noble Capua is reflected in the waters of the Volturno. Set in a loop of the river, the town rose on the site of a small Roman river port.

161 bottom The Castello delle Pietre at Capua, also known as the Palace of the Norman Princes, was built with blocks of stone from the ancient Campano Amphitheater.

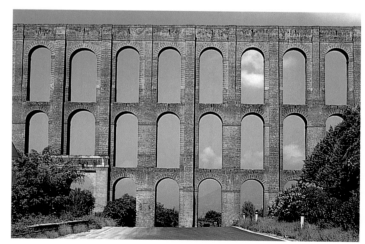

overlooking the terracing. The Lombards used it as a fortress, and the marble and most precious furnishings were stripped to construct roads and palaces. The Capua of today is a few miles away, enclosed in a loop of the Volturno, a veritable treasure chest of history. There are the Roman ruins, the medieval quarter and the Lombard churches, the towers and the gate that, designed personally by Frederick II of Swabia, became the symbolic entrance to the south of Italy, the fifteenth century palace of Rinaldo Fieramosca, father of the famous Ettore who defended Barletta, the sixteenth century bastions of

the Spanish viceroy's stronghold, and the Duomo, destroyed and rebuilt a number of times between 800 and the present day. Here, five centuries before Christ, the women invoked the goddess of fertility and, having produced numerous strong and healthy children, offered votive images sculpted in stone of mothers proudly displaying their new-born babies.

Behind the city stand the high Matese mountains, snow-capped in winter, with their lakes. The Apennines lead towards the Sannio region, in the province of Benevento, skirting Irpinia, province of Avellino.

162-163 The houses of Sant'Agata de'Goti overlook the deep gorge of one of the two tributaries of the River Isclero surrounding the small village that grew up on the site of the town of Saticula, founded during the Samnite period.

162 bottom An unusual and broad flight of curving steps leads to the entrance of the eighteenth century church of San Martino at Cerreto Sannita. This small town is known for the craft traditions of its fabrics and ceramics.

Following the course of the water carried to the royal palace in reverse, the road climbs through gentle green hills, slips between higher mountains, and approaches the vineyards producing the fine wine of Solopaca and Taurasi, beyond the gorge of the Arpaia where the Samnite's ambush at the Forche Caudine succeeded in the daring plan to defeat the Roman army. In the valleys and on the slopes of the mountains there are towns and villages condemned by history and geography to an isolation of centuries and impoverishment due to widespread emigration as thousands and thousands of young people left in search of fortune in distant lands. Here, where the traditional methods of working the land endures, the countryside defends rituals and flavors that have disappeared elsewhere and life flows slowly.

They are simple villages with just a few houses. The towns have a style that betrays a different, richer history. They were home to the feudal lords or bishops who imposed the might of the Church of Rome. The houses of Sant'Agata dei Goti appear to be balanced on the crest of a steep spur of rock extending between the valleys excavated by two tributaries of the River Isclero. A Samnite and Roman city, subsequently under the control of the Goths and then Byzantium, it boasts a Lombard castle, a suggestive historic center rich in art, churches, and palaces that recall the presence of Sant'Alfonso de'Liguori and the power of an

163 right Agriculture characterizes the countryside around Cusano Mutri where the land is covered not only with woods but also orchards and cultivated fields, a landscape typical of the mountains around Benevento.

important diocese.

The houses of Cusano Mutri climb with great arches on the living rock of Mount Mutria. Redesigned three centuries ago after a disastrous earthquake, Cerreto Sannita has since remained unchanged. It contains broad, grid-pattern avenues, attractive buildings, the cathedral, a suggestive flight of steps leading to the church of San Martino, the and enduring craft traditions of making fine cloth and ceramic plates and amphorae with characteristic coloring and designs. Unfortunately, traditional arts risk disappearing and from town to

164 left In the grape picking season the craftsmen of Solopaca, a village known for the fine wine of the same name, build large allegorical floats that, completely covered with bunches of grapes, parade on the day of the Festa dell'Uva. Building the floats is a long and painstaking task that is undertaken with passion. Carefully placing one grape next to another, the heirs of this ancient tradition create minor masterpieces.

town just a few workshops defend the heritage of the master smiths' wrought iron work and the women's lace-making.

In Benevento and the small towns in the province nougat-like sweet **torrone** is made and has been famous for centuries. Using honey, almonds, and liqueur in a classic recipe, a heart of sponge soaked in liqueur becomes the **torrone** of the small village makers. There is also **torroncino**, made with fragments of almonds in caramelized sugar with a chocolate coating. Those of San Marco dei Cavoti are known throughout the world. Thus does each town and village cling to its own traditions. There are still strong ties between religion and the rhythms and alternating fortunes of agriculture as demonstrated by thanksgiving festivals and processions during the **vendemmia** or grape picking season or the autumn harvest. In Solopaca, floats covered with thousands of bunches of red grapes parade for the Festa dell'Uva, or Festival of the Grape, and in nearby Irpinia, at Mirabella Eclano, on the day of the Festa del Carro, or Festival of the Wagon, the townsfolk carry a great obelisk weighing 20 tons on their shoulders around the fields in tribute to Our Lady of Sorrows. At Guardia Sanframondi an ancient ritual is practiced that is shocking in the crudity of the gestures dictated by extremist faith. Every seven years the "beaters" run up and down the streets of the old town, below the castle, wearing hoods and long white tunics that soon become red with blood as they repeatedly beat their legs and chests with sponges soaked in vinegar concealing thorns and piece of glass. In the meantime the town prays and in procession offers the sacrifice of its citizens to Our Lady of the Assumption. Modern-day history leads hundreds of pilgrims to Pietrelcina, the home town of the blessed Padre Pio.

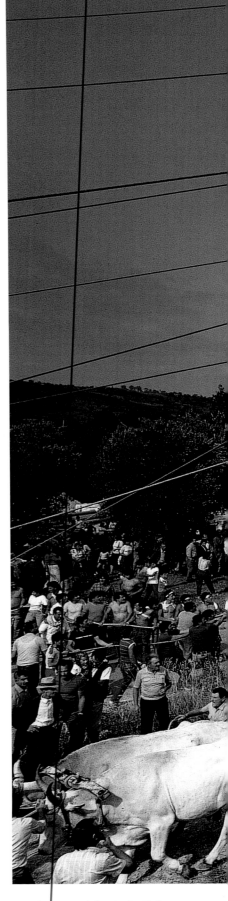

164-165 A tall obelisk, made of straw woven into beautiful decorative motifs is hauled by oxen each September along the twisting country lanes. The Festa del Carro at Mirabella Eclano, set among the mountains of Irpinia, is one of the most evocative of the traditional country fairs.

165 bottom left The flavorsome annurche apples typical of Maddaloni and neighboring villages in the Benevento area are picked while still sour and stored one beside another on beds of straw. They then mature thanks to the patience of the farmer's wives whose task it is to turn them frequently, one by one.

165 bottom right Lake Telese occupies a small volcanic crater. The surrounding area is known for its thermal springs that were already gushing when, in 1349, a terrible earthquake destroyed the village of Telesia, the heir to a small Roman town.

Benevento is set in a green hollow between the rivers Sabato and Calore. This is the Terra delle Streghe, or Land of Witches, but the suggestive legends that tell of a place elected for rituals and covens does not do justice to a city that boasts many important points of historical interest. The grand Triumphal Arch, today the symbolic gateway to Benevento, is a symbol of the power of Rome. It was erected at the behest of the emperor Trajan in 114 to celebrate the opening of the section of the Via Appia that from here, by way of Lucania and Puglia, led towards the port of Brundusium and opened up to the empire the Adriatic routes to the East. The trading route was a source of great wealth. The arch, with its bas-reliefs, is a vainglorious folly consigned to history. It recounts and hands down the acts, virtues, victories, and good deeds of the emperor, his relationship with Rome and Benevento, and the magnanimous gesture of distributing bread to the poor children. The monumental Roman Theater was the work of Hadrian. Today, as in the distant past, it is the setting for open-air entertainment, classical tragedies, and opera performances. The medieval church of Santa Sofia, with the Benedictine convent and its beautiful cloister, recalls the years of the powerful Lombard duchy. It was built at the behest of Arechi II, the last duke of Benevento and the first prince of a dominion that after having ruled the city for two hundred years expanded its sphere of influence to include almost all of southern Italy. In a mosaic of stone decipcting scenes from history, the elegant Duomo, dating from the seventh century but rebuilt a number of times, bears Lombard funerary inscriptions set in the facade and Roman marble work in the massive campanile.

A shy provincial city that has never wholly overcome its a penalizing geographical isolation, it is nonetheless a lively center of culture and the home of successful theatrical programs. Benevento does not flaunt its jewels and is only marginally touched by the tourist routes. It is still waiting to be discovered. The fourteenth century Rocca dei Rettori was once a fortress defending the Benedictine convent and then a prison. Called "the castle," it now houses the relics of the Museo del Sannio, the museum that recounts the history of this area from the monuments to the secrets of the narrow streets of the old town that spread out from Corso Garibaldi below the walls of the fortress.

166 The majestic Arch of Trajan is a symbol of Benevento's past glory. Dating back to the year 114, it was erected in honor of the emperor who had supported the project of extending the Via Appia as far as the port of Brindisi, passing by way of the Samnite city.

167 top right and top left The campanile of Santa Sofia stands isolated in the historic center of Benevento. The church, a mediaeval masterpiece, is a short distance away. It was founded in 762 by Arechi II when he became duke of the city. At the center of the piazza the obelisk of the fountain rests on four lions.

167 top center The Rocca dei Rettori was built on the highest point in Benevento. It is in part composed of the fourteenth century "Manfredi" castle built on the ruins of a Lombard fortress.

167 bottom center Today, as at the time of the emperor Hadrian, music and prose are staged in the second century Roman theater and the great cavea is filled with spectators on summer evenings in Benevento.

167 bottom This white marble lion carved during the reign of Emperor Severus ornaments the Roman theater in Benevento.

168-169 From the sanctuary of Montevergine, which stands on the summit of a hill behind Avellino, the view ranges over the woods and villages of the Irpinia region. The houses of Ospedaletto d'Alpinolo stand out against the green of the Irpinian slopes.

168 bottom The white sanctuary of Madonna delle Grazie stands at the foot of Mount Terminio at Serino, in the chestnut forests typical of this part of the Irpinia region.

The shyness of provincial cities slightly intimidated by the pomp of Naples, and the beautiful countryside with its hill towns set amid green woods, are characteristics also encountered at Avellino and its surroundings. This is the heart of Campania. Here there are vineyards and good wine and the typical sight of large tobacco leaves cultivated on every small plot of land, hung neatly to dry in the open air, from the frames of large wooden barns with a roof but no walls.

The dense chestnut woods climb up the mountain slopes. These are the proud possession of Montella, a town famous for its superb chestnuts. Truffles are also gathered in the woods. Those found in the mountains behind Bagnoli are renowned. The economy is intimately tied to the countryside, with the minor exceptions of perhaps a couple of towns where the heritage of age-old traditions has become the driving force behind industrial concerns. Among the mountains, Solofra, a minor capital of the tanning industry, features innumerable tanneries and leather tailoring businesses.

During the evening of November 23, 1980, the earth began to shake, erasing history. It was a severe, mortal blow for Sant'Angelo dei Lombardi, Lioni, Conza, Torella, and Laviano. The people counted their dead, over three thousand, with ten thousand injured and a hundred thousand homeless. Families were torn from their simple lives rooted in the ancient parishes. Ghost towns were created, and for fifteen years life continued in the cold encampments of prefabricated houses. Today, many old villages have literally disappeared. A few stones, the occasional campanile, and a few old walls remain among the houses of cities reborn through urgent and ugly speculative building, deep scars on the landscape and in the hearts of the people. Life is no longer that of the agricultural workers who lived in the evocative stone houses in the lanes of little villages set around a church.

However, the beautiful, unspoiled landscape and a few historical treasures endure. The green of the Picentini mountain park and the towering Mount Terminio and the ring of peaks around Lake Laceno where people ski in winter testify to the region's natural beauty. Traces of the important historical heritage can be found in Atripalda, overlooking the River Sabato, at the Christian cemetery of the ancient Abellinum founded by Sulla, and at the church of Sant'Ippolito built on the hypogeum where the remains of the saint and the martyr victims of the persecution ordered by the emperor Diocletian were piously gathered. A few walls of the old castle in medieval Grottaminarda still stand as well as some patrician houses and thermal baths at Passo di Mirabella and the Roman Aeclanum. Christian catacombs and the apse carved into the tuff of the Church of Our Lady of the Annunciation exist at Prata di Principato Ultra. The centuries-old abbey of San Gugliemo at Golteo has towering walls overlooking the River Ofanto. Guardi dei Lombardi rises noble and proud on a hill around the sixteenth century church of Santa Maria delle Grazie.

The earthquake did not spare Avellino. The city, however, proved capable of gritting its teeth and

169 top For years the cultivation of tobacco—which is hung to dry in great wooden barns—has been one of the principal resources of the countryside between Caserta and Benevento. This practice still survives today although it is now in decline.

169 bottom Vigorous chestnut trees cloak great areas of Mount Terminio. In the summer this is an enchanting picnic and walking destination.

170 top left The sanctuary of Montevergine, overlooking the Avellino valley from a limestone crag in the Partendo range, is crowded with devout pilgrims.

170 bottom left The acacia trees raise their elegant branches to the sky in the Villa Communale of Avellino. There is no lack of greenery in this city surrounded by forest-covered mountains.

hanging on tenaciously when the first shops to reopen were housed in freezing huts and families in prefabs houses waited for the day in which, years and years later, they were able to return to their homes. It is a modern city. Well before the coup de grâce delivered by the quake of 1980, the disastrous aerial bombardment of 1943 had left little trace of the of the oldest history apart from a few ruins of the Lombard castle. Little of the flourishing years under the Caracciolo princes, from the end of the sixteenth century to a little over two hundred years later remained. The Duomo, rebuilt a century ago, conceals an older secret: the crypt of Santa Maria dei Sette Dolori dating from 1100. Among the eighteenth century frescoes and the Roman capitals emerge the works of the original Lombard cathedral.

The last few years have seen great movement towards rebirth, determination, and a show of pride. Day by day the city appears more attractive, lively once again. The gardens between the gushing fountains of Piazza della Libertà are flourishing. The citizens walk up and down in front of the shop windows on Corso Vittorio Emanuele, a meeting place when the sun goes down during the summer and a breath of wind descends from the ring of mountains surrounding the city. This is the hour of the ritual passeggiata, or stroll. Up from the highest peak, in the woods of the Partenio Park, below the bare rock summit, the Sanctuary of Montevergine protects Benevento with its benevolent gaze. This tribute to the Virgin Mary was built at the behest of Guglielmo di Vercelli in 1100.

Faith and popular tradition combine, in an atmosphere that marries the sacred and the profane. A million pilgrims each year render homage to "Mamma Schiavona," the image portrayed in a great fourteenth century tablet. Visiting the Shrine is a ritual for the people of Campania. The route climbs through green woods before emerging in a square where a group of stalls sell torrone and gadgets, toys and sweets, crafts and mementoes. At the entrance the collection of the votive offerings left by those whose prayers have been answered is displayed. Then there is the traditional visit to the treasures of the Chiesa Vecchia (the Old Church) and the monastery and the great Chiesa Nuova (New Church), built fifty years ago to increase the space available for such a constant stream of pilgrims. Great celebrations are held on San Guglielmo's day, the twenty-fifth of June and on the traditional Italian holiday of Ferragosto, the fifteenth of August, in a blend of religion and folklore.

170-171 The large Piazza della Libertà is the heart of Avellino's historic city center. The eighteenth century palace of the Caracciolo Princes overlooks fountains surrounded by ornamental gardens.

171 bottom Roman and medieval capitals decorate the small chapel of Santa Maria dei Sette Dolori, also known as the Crypt of Our Lady of Sorrows. Of Norman origins but rebuilt in the seventeenth century, the chapel is located in the undercroft of Avellino's

cathedral. Alongside stucco-work and frescoed walls, there are visible remains of the original Romanesque structure where, between great blocks of stone one can see epigraphs and decorations taken from the funerary monuments of the Roman town.

172 top left The elegant campanile decorated with entwined arches faces onto the porticoed atrium of the cathedral of Salerno in an original blend of Byzantine and Islamic motifs frequently seen along the Amalfitana coast.

172 bottom left Ancient Roman sarcophagi have been used for a number of tombs in the lateral naves of the Duomo, where columns and arches reveal the original Romanesque style. The great church was built at the behest of Roberto I Guiscardo and the archbishop Alfano, Abbot of Montecassino.

172-173 The castle of Arechi II stands on the green hill of Salerno. The historic city center with its treasures sits at the foot of the hill. A short distance away are the new residential developments and the port.

173 top right The great tiered arches of the Salerno aqueduct date back to the eighth century and were restored by the Normans.

173 bottom An elegant loggia faces onto two sides of the large atrium giving access to the Duomo. The quadrilateral portico with round arches features 28 granite columns from the Roman period.

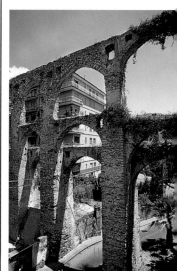

Skirting to the east the mountains of Lucania and Irpinia encounter the province of Salerno, the region's most extensive, running south for mile after mile. Salerno is lapped by the waters of the broad bay that the Greeks called Posidonia and the Romans Paestanus. A few miles to the north, the beauty of the Amalfitana coast leads towards Punta Campanella. Heading south, the ancient ruins of Paestum rise before the coast of Campania ends at the lighthouse on Punta Licosa in the heart of the Cilento shoreline.

Among hills, the sea, history, and the beautiful landscape, the city of Salerno synthesizes the riches of its land, presenting two distinct and distant faces. It is a city that experiences indirectly the intensive tourism of the province's coasts and enjoys the growth of a solid economy based on the transit of goods through its large commercial port. However, it also boasts a rich history. The Via dei Mercanti, beyond an old arch, runs between the lands of the old town clinging to the hill, dominated by the great Arechi castle which was inhabited throughout changing dynasties, from the Lombards to the Normans to the Aragonese.

The new town stretches elegantly behind the palm-shaded Trieste Promenade, the Villa Comunale, the nineteenth century Teatro Verdi, the palaces of the city's political and business center, the tourist port, and the more modern quarters creatively remodeled by the Catalan urban planner Oriol Bohigas.

The golden age of Salerno was the Medieval period, the Duomo being the most impressive example. Dedicated to Our Lady of the Assumption, it was born as a "house" for the wandering remains of Matthew the Evangelist, brought to Velia by Calabrian sailors, then hurriedly transported to Lucania to keep them out of reach of marauding Saracen pirates, then to Paestum, and finally to Salerno where the Norman Roberto il Guiscardo, after having taken the city by storm, followed the advice of the Lombard bishop, Alfano, and had a church built that was worthy of such an important tomb. Extraordinarily beautiful, it represents perhaps the most important of the examples of high medieval sacred architecture in southern Italy.

The Romanesque style has survived here, although not without being subjected to the Baroque influences of more recent years. Among the oldest treasures, of particular note are the tombs built around ancient Roman sarcophagi. Queen Margherita of Durazzo rests here.

Years of wealth, are confirmed by the churches and palaces of the old town. Of that time history records the prestige of the School of Salerno, the oldest and most important medical academy in the west.

174 top left and bottom A wall of colored containers covers the pier in the commercial port of Salerno. Ships come and go in what is an increasingly important international trading port, *but there is also a continuous stream of elegant yachts and small boats. The marina is in fact always crowded, in part because it is but a short voyage from here to the sights of the Amalfitana coast.*

174-175 *Salerno is embraced by the broad bay of the same name which stretches from the Amalfitana to the Cilento coasts. There is a close relationship between the city and its sea, historically and currently. Apart from tourism, with the marina and fine beaches virtually in the town center, there is also a fishing tradition and a major commercial port.*

175 bottom *A slim strip of green divides the new town from the sea. Among the trees, numerous palms help create a sophisticated atmosphere for the Trieste sea-front at Salerno.*

176 *The Sorrentine coast closes the Bay of Naples to the south, over which looms the imposing, threatening Vesuvius.*

AIR CONCESSION
Concession S. M. A. n. 1-634 of 04/11/1997